REPRESENTATION AND CITIZENSHIP

SERIES IN CITIZENSHIP STUDIES

SERIES EDITORS

Marc W. Kruman
Richard Marback

REPRESENTATION AND CITIZENSHIP

·········

EDITED BY RICHARD MARBACK

Wayne State University Press
Detroit

© 2016 by Wayne State University Press, Detroit, Michigan 48201.
All rights reserved. No part of this book may be reproduced without formal permission.
Manufactured in the United States of America.

20 19 18 17 16   5 4 3 2 1

Library of Congress Control Number: 2016945437
ISBN 978-0-8143-4246-6 (paperback)
ISBN 978-0-8143-4247-3 (ebook)

∞

Designed and typeset by Bryce Schimanski
Composed in Adode Caslon Pro

CONTENTS

INTRODUCTION

· · · · · · · · · ·

RICHARD MARBACK

Concern with representation figures inescapably in the study of citizenship. From the initial formulations of a notion of citizenship in ancient Greece, in which citizens were persons charged with representing the interests of the city-state, concern about who and what gets represented, as well as how and why those people and things get represented, have been central in formulas describing the citizen's relationship to a political community. From these ancient roots we have retained the view that a citizen is, at least in part, someone whose participation in such things as public deliberation, jury duty, and military service represents through those acts the interests of the larger community of which he or she is a member. For the ancient Athenians, as Aristotle tells us, such an ideal citizen, one who puts aside private interest for the sake of the public good, did not expect the concerns of the community as a whole to be representative of his individual interests. The Athenian citizen understood that, through his participation in public affairs, he represented not himself but the polis. He was in this sense an embodiment of public interests, his words and deeds figuring forth the larger interests of the political community to which he pledged himself. Plato gave this view of citizenship its most forceful expression in the *Republic*, where he described the education of the guardian class as an education in which the souls of the rulers are brought into alignment with the order of the state so that they could learn to embody in themselves the interests of the polis. Whatever fault we

I

may find with Plato's guardian class, we can recognize how the democratic aspirations of Athenian citizenship, surrendering self-interest for public good, evolved over time from the rule of Solon (ca. 640–559 BCE), who extended citizenship status beyond the ranks of the aristocracy, to that of Pericles (ca. 490–429 BCE), who democratized the appointment of archons by opening it to citizens other than the Athenian elite.

In one sense, then, significant developments in Athenian citizenship turned on expanding and encouraging more and more citizens to take on roles as representatives of community interests that largely displaced their individual interests. Subsequent elaborations of citizenship in terms of either ideals or experiences of representation came to turn as well on reformulating the relationship of citizens and their private interests to the interests of the polity as a whole. Significant in this regard, in the seventeenth century, the status of citizen came to be formulated as a guarantee of noninterference by the state in the citizen's private affairs, a guarantee that, in the American and French revolutions of the eighteenth century, sets the sovereignty of citizens as a measure of the legitimacy of governments. Such an understanding of citizens as possessing inalienable rights to their private property, rights the state is bound to protect, quickly finds elaboration in the idea of government as a means for representing the aggregation of property interests in collective political action. An important consequence that follows from understanding collective interests as an aggregation of individual interests is a reciprocal comprehension of individual citizens in terms of the political community as a whole. Where in ancient Athens the interests of the state become the interests of the citizen, here in the American and French revolutions the interests of citizens have become the interest of the state.

Since the seventeenth century the tension between citizens as representatives of the interests of the state and the state as representative of the interests of its citizens has found practical and theoretical elaborations in understandings and exercises of citizenship. Today, the concept of representation resonates widely within citizenship studies, and its generative ambiguity gives expression to many of the key issues of community membership, creating in this way a critical vocabulary through which those issues can be expressed. It is this vocabulary of representation that this volume addresses. Here I explore some of the resonances of representation in order to provide a context for the chapters that follow. To preview what follows, these chapters can be read as organized around two concerns with representation that do—but do not necessarily have to—pull against each other: the one aligned with appeals to foundations as these are engaged in Rogers Smith's contribution to this volume, the other aligned with notions of multiculturalism as these are discussed in Will Kymlicka's contribution to this volume. Taken together, the contributions of Smith and Kymlicka circumscribe issues of representation that the remaining chapters of this volume address.

I begin with the appeals to a political community's origins, appeals that form the foundations for that community's sense of shared values. In his contribution to this collection, "Lincoln and Obama: Two Visions of Civic Union," Rogers Smith notes Obama's appeals to Lincoln to make the case for both presidents sharing commitment to a tradition of American constitutionalism and to the union, "but only insofar as they can be seen, on balance and over time, to be contributing to realizing the commitments of the Declaration of Independence, that all humanity should enjoy the basic liberties of life, liberty, and the pursuit of happiness, including rights of free labor" (32). Grounding bonds of citizenship on recognition of shared commitments to individual pursuits of happiness is unmistakably a matter of representation. As Smith makes clear, the successes of both Lincoln and Obama turn on their capacities for forging an image of America that fosters—to the degree possible—the collective commitments of the nation's citizens, with the successes of Lincoln's "nineteenth-century natural rights liberalism" and Obama's "modern democratic pragmatism" turning on "Lincoln's insistence on certain moral absolutes over Obama's hopes for consensual, deliberative, evolving multiculturalism" (45). To put it in terms of representation, the political success of these two presidents reveals the essential tension through which citizens can come to recognize that their interests are represented within a larger representation of American constitutionalism. As Smith concludes, "inclusive democratic unity may not always be the nation's highest goal. . . . Leaders must sometimes try to speak, not primarily to Americans as they are, but to the better angels of their nature, if their nation is to be stirred to pursue forms of civic union more perfect than those achieved so far" (46).

Of course the challenge to such an aspirational politics is not only the challenge of winning collective commitment, it is also the challenge of mobilizing that commitment to fashion an identity for those who count as citizens with a stake in their state's vision of the common good that all share. Will Kymlicka addresses these concerns in his contribution to this volume, "Trajectories of Multicultural Citizenship." In his essay Kymlicka traces

3

narratives of the rise and fall of multiculturalism in order to propose a different narrative, one that finds hope for multicultural agendas. Where narratives of multiculturalism have faltered on a tolerance of differences that can perpetuate stereotypes, gloss over the complexity of cultural values, and ignore inequalities, narratives of, what Kymlicka calls, post-multiculturalists respond by prioritizing equality of political participation, economic opportunity, and human rights. Both the multiculturalists and the post-multiculturalists have their points. Both also, as Kymlicka argues, only tell half the story of multiculturalism in its more robust form:

> In the past, it was often assumed that the only way to engage in this process of citizenization was to impose a single undifferentiated model of citizenship on all individuals. But the ideas and policies of multiculturalism that emerged from the 1960s start from the assumption that this complex history inevitably and appropriately generates group-differentiated ethnopolitical claims. The key to citizenization is not to suppress these differentiated claims, but to filter and frame them through the language of human rights, civil liberties, and democratic accountability. And this is what multiculturalist movements have aimed to do. (59)

Reading Kymlicka's claim in terms of a dynamics of representation, we could say that human rights, civil liberties, and democratic accountability serve as guiding principles for states in which citizens justly represent and acknowledge within their political community the range of their individually held cultural values. This is not to say that any and all cultural values matter in a political community or that any and all values merit respect from a political community. It is instead to second Kymlicka in saying that the struggles for recognition of minorities and indigenous peoples are "about restructuring state institutions, including redistributing political control over important public and natural resources" (61). At their core, as Kymlicka makes clear with reference to the redistribution of political control, struggles for restructuring institutions so that they redistribute resources more fairly are struggles for political representation.

Another point made clear by Kymlicka's appeal for the redistribution of political control is that decisions about inclusion and exclusion that are made in terms of representation have at their core concern about resources.

Understandably, concerns with who gets what, concerns with access to such things as attention, benefits, obligations, power, rights, resources, and services, are among the primary concerns citizens have in their day-to-day affairs. The limits, both real and imagined, that constrain the availability of access to entitlements push questions of who gets what into deliberations about not only distribution but also representation. Debates over the availability of and access to health care resources, for example, ask people to delimit from all available medical care the kinds of access that do and do not constitute the basic health care all members of a community should have. When the costs are low, it is easier to find broad agreement on basic health care. Programs providing easy access to insulin for all diabetics are a good example of low-cost care for which broad public support could be more easily generated. As costs go up, and as medical resources become more scarce, it is easy to imagine agreement becoming more difficult. We should not be surprised, for example, to find less agreement over public funding for prohibitively expensive treatments, such as organ transplants, for complications arising from diabetes. Among the arguments citizens—as well as their legislative representatives—can have against public funding for such costly medical procedures, we often hear reference to age ("he is too old") or lifestyle ("she didn't take enough care of her health") or even character ("who is he to deserve this?") and obligation ("why should I pay for her procedure?") as well as membership ("he is not a citizen"). Here we can see how the question "who gets what?" has become a question of "who is what?," a question that asks people to stake their claims regarding entitlements and obligations in terms of representations of themselves that identify who they are for each other and to each other. To characterize in this way the relationship between access and identity is not to suggest that issues of allocation reduce to matters of representation; it is instead to draw attention to the fact that the daily concerns of citizens emerge and unfold through the dynamics of representation.

We begin to fathom the pervasive power that representations of citizenship have in our lives by focusing on the lived experience of claims to community membership and by considering how those claims of identity are presentations of the self as a person in the world who is asking for recognition. Appeals for recognition that make claims on a community's resources, for example, are a person's request for recognition as a citizen of a community. To gain recognition from others—to have them accept our representations of ourselves as fellow citizens—we must make our identities apparent to them. Our presentations of ourselves cannot be so idiosyncratic, so out of keeping with what others expect, as to be either invisible or indecipherable. In our presentations of ourselves we must to the degree necessary adopt representations that have already been established and that others find familiar enough. This is not to say that we are left to present ourselves only in the manner others expect, knowing within what our true nature really is. The dynamics of representation, of self-perception and social presentation, are not so easily reducible to the opposition of internal reality and external appearance. Who we perceive ourselves to be cannot but emerge and evolve through our interactions with others. With regards to our identities as citizens, those interactions are inescapably institutionalized, including everything from schooling, to commerce, to travel, and even international athletic competitions. Over the course of lives lived through institutionalized relationships we have the opportunity to reflect on ourselves and our interactions with others. In the process of our reflections we become aware of, and come to make choices about, who we perceive ourselves to be, who we perceive others to be, as well as how we want others to perceive us. We may all of us recognize ourselves as citizens of a given state at the same time that we surely do disagree in significant ways about what is entailed in counting someone as a citizen. Implications and issues following from awareness of the tension between, on the one hand, demands for and identification with a political community and, on the other hand, individual differences in experiences of identification are the central concern of this collection of essays.

To be clear, the concern is not one of creating institutions capable of aligning our identifications in ways that overcome our differences. Even when our relationships are structured by inclusive or forgiving institutions, the dynamic process of engagement through which others recognize us and we experience ourselves as perceived is a process as generative of misrecognition as it is of recognition. Failures of recognition, such as when we experience ourselves as either misunderstood by or inscrutable or invisible to others, are failures of association that can generate within us what W. E. B. Du Bois aptly termed "double consciousness," an internal dissonance between how I perceive myself and what I experience as my reception by others. The damaging effects of double consciousness are particularly pernicious for those persons marginalized or excluded from meaningful participation in a community because they are perceived as so different that others cannot imagine them having a role in the life of a community. In their extreme forms, those persons come to imagine themselves as useless. Exclusions based on perceptions of differences such as those of ability, ethnicity, race, gender, sexual orientation, or religious affiliation have been revealed again and again as arbitrary and illegitimate constraints on the participation of citizens. Despite serious problems within political communities of unjust exclusions that have been grounded in a politics of identity and difference, identity politics has still figured centrally as the means for many people who have experienced exclusion or marginalization to assert their civic membership.

We need only recall the successes of the American civil rights movement, the disabilities movement, and the women's movement to remind ourselves of successes in enlarging the boundaries of citizenship. At the same time, responses of retrenchment to the greater inclusions won through identity politics caution us about the challenges posed by human diversity to our aspirations for inclusive communities.

From the fact that there is too often a mismatch between experiences of self and recognition of that self by others, Patchen Markell has argued for replacing a politics of identity with a politics of acknowledgment, a politics that "does not confuse justice in relations of identity and difference with mutual transparency, or with security from risk, or with the overcoming of all experiences of alienation or even hostility in our relations with others" (Markell 2003, 7). To use Markell's terms, when others acknowledge our presence as fellow citizens we have not only affirmed a sense of ourselves in relation to those others, we have also thereby enmeshed ourselves in a community of shared concern. What we have not done is made ourselves transparent as members of a community and so available to each other in mutually agreed upon terms. Markell's proposal for a politics of acknowledgment draws its virtue from the fact that the idealized politics of mutual identification are dissonant with human experience. As humans we never exist outside community and we typically experience ourselves as bound to multiple communities at any given moment in our lives—among them families, friends, fellow hobbyists, civic organizations, and political parties. We belong to and feel the pull of communities that draw on our connectedness to locations, kin, interests, and nationalities.

Interactions structured through overlapping communities, from the local to the global, cannot but shape us and our senses of ourselves. To paraphrase the African adage, we become who we are in our relationships with those persons we are closest to. The unfolding through time of identities, concerns, and communities is a constant process of making and remaking representations of self, one of which is representation of the self as citizen. This point has been made again and again across the theoretical and political spectrum, by communitarians such as Michael Sandel, liberals such as John Rawls, and Marxists such as Louis Althusser. While communitarians, liberals, and Marxists may dispute what it means for us to represent ourselves to each other as citizens, they are in general agreement that it is through representation, when people successfully acknowledge each other as fellow citizens, that those people make the strongest possible claims for their access to a community's public entitlements.

We further confirm the intimate connection between representations of citizenship and distribution of resources by reflecting on the fact that denials of claims of a citizenship identity have long been used to exclude others who are identified as noncitizens from their access to the limited resources of public entitlements. While such exclusions may have their place in drawing the boundaries of a community's shared concerns, they also raise questions about the justice of representations of citizenship, as when undocumented immigrants and their children are denied access to basic health benefits because they are not recognized as citizens. To children of undocumented immigrants who have lived their entire lives in a given country, the claim that they are not citizens and that they are therefore denied entitlements often contradicts their sense of themselves as members of that community. No doubt their struggles for citizenship and all its entitlements aspire to such tangible things as health care, but these are struggles carried on in the name of gaining acknowledgment as citizens.

Prominent examples such as the struggle against apartheid in South Africa, or the struggle for civil rights in the United States, demonstrate that acquiring full citizenship status involves more than being able to claim inclusion on terms already established by a community. Successful struggles against exclusion and for inclusion entail revisions of representations through which the boundaries of a community are drawn and identity claims get made. While some revisions of representations of citizenship are quite dramatic—such as in the end of apartheid in South Africa—the absence of continuous revolution should not lull us into believing the process of transformation ever stops. Consider how in the half century since the height of the civil rights movement in the United States representations of citizenship have gotten entangled with concerns over entitlements in ways few would have then anticipated. Supreme Court decisions from *Brown* to *Bakke* to *Grutter* and *Gratz* have enabled remedies for the injustices of racial discrimination in access to schooling while over time narrowing the concern with discrimination to a matter of individual injury, thereby tipping the scales of justice away from concern for shared experiences of historically entrenched racial attitudes toward established meritocratic privilege. Similarly, in the Roberts's Court's recent ruling on the Voting Rights Act of 1965, federal protections against racial discrimination in voting are characterized as outdated and unnecessary, a misrecognition and misrepresentation of the status of African Americans as citizens.

Retreat from affirmative action and from the Voting Rights Act signals an end point to a logic of identity politics that emerged in the 1970s out of the civil rights struggles of the 1960s. Identity politics was no doubt productively critical of exclusions on the basis of group differences, successfully making the case for inclusion of differences without assimilation of the identities of those different groups. Today, however, the strongest claims for appeals for acknowledgment of differences are claims for justice expressed in terms of multiculturalism. Multiculturalism highlights the value that difference has, not only in the life of the individual, but in the life of the community as well. A multicultural perspective begins with acknowledgment of the fact that people come into their identities as citizens through their rich and varied experiences of their ethnicity, their gender, and their heritage, to name but a few. Appeals for citizenship that ground in experiences of being different from others—whether that difference is one of ethnicity, gender, or religion—necessarily enlarge the range of possible appeals citizens can make for access to a community's resources as well as identification with the common concerns of others in their community.

Certainly, the expansion of the basis for citizenship claims has inherent within it a number of contentions. More than this, in terms of claims for redistribution of resources that ground in appeals to a recognition of differences, Nancy Fraser has discerned a further dilemma. As Fraser has argued, claims for recognition and resources based on appeals to difference, such as in affirmative action admissions to public universities, have the potential to elicit resentment from others unable to make such appeals because their identities prohibit it. According to Fraser the result is not only an appearance of inequality but more importantly a possible stigmatizing of those differences upon which claims for redistribution of resources are made (Fraser

2003, 65). While Fraser's characterization of the relationship between recognition and redistribution has received a good deal of critical attention, the point here is that appeals to multiculturalism, as productive as they have been in enlarging terms of inclusion, have not, for the reasons Kymlicka makes clear in his contribution to this volume, successfully met all the challenges of delimiting just distribution. Those appeals to multiculturalism have instead, as Fraser points out, been met with the kind of retrenchment that has been the fate of affirmative action in the United States.

While there is no denying resistance to multicultural inclusivity and cosmopolitan openness, it would be a mistake to describe the retreat from affirmative action as the resurgence of a foundational ideology. As much as efforts to fight affirmative action in the United States may be waged with reference to a fidelity to the intent of the founding fathers and to the text of the Constitution, such efforts by themselves do not make those appeals to original intent or those references to founding documents either legitimate or accurate representations of the nation's origins. The beliefs and values through which the United States took its fledgling form are not available to us through a literal interpretation of such founding documents as the Declaration of Independence and the original Constitution. In debates over just how citizens today ought to interpret these documents, a case could be made that the imperatives of multicultural inclusivity and cosmopolitan openness are legitimate expansions of the ideology upon which the United States was founded. As such, debates over differences in interpretation of foundational documents, whether to read them liberally or literally, are debates about representation in the sense that what is at stake are matters of representing to ourselves what the boundaries of our shared concerns are and who is included in those concerns.

As I have tried to show in this brief introduction, concerns with who gets included and who gets excluded are never settled once and for all. It is not simply that each generation of citizens is a generation further removed from the immediate force of a community's founding ideology. It is also that each generation of citizens is made up of more and more people whose representations to themselves and to each other merit our acknowledgment. Each generation of citizens must face its own challenges, and each must decide how it is to be guided by its representations in that task.

The chapters collected in this volume take on the pull of identification with a community's founding ideology on the one hand and, on the other, assertions for inclusion of multicultural differences. This is not to suggest that identification and inclusion persist as our only options. To be clear, articulating issues of citizenship in terms of acknowledging the push and pull of representations creates an opportunity for moving beyond the binary opposition of founding ideologies—understood as setting boundaries of exclusion—and multicultural ideologies—understood as making claims for expanding the boundaries of inclusion. Instead, as the contributions to this volume show, the dialogue between the articulation of a founding ideology and assertions of the values that attach to diversity is more productively generative of greater nuance in representations of our civic identities.

Appeals to cosmopolitan norms, for example, expand the circle of a community's concerns beyond foundational ideologies, according respect for differences without grounding claims for resource redistribution in terms of those differences. Cosmopolitanism accepts differences of ourselves from others as fundamental to the human condition, in this way shifting the ground for representing to ourselves just what our foundational ideology can be. Rather than highlighting those differences as grounds for appeals, cosmopolitanism places its emphasis on the relationships of people to each other. By virtue of the fundamental differences that exist between persons, our interactions with each other are always potentially generative: We develop our identities through our encounters with others who are different from us and so who challenge the limits of our experiences and perspectives.

While cosmopolitan norms may avoid the stigmatizing of minority rights claims, those norms are not for this reason without their problems. As beings who interact more with those closest to us, we can have difficulty imagining the worth of relationships to those persons furthest from us. It is here that the construction of national boundaries and national identities generates patriotic loyalty to founding ideologies. Despite the identification of citizenship interests with national boundaries, Martha Nussbaum, among others, has argued that patriotism and cosmopolitanism need not remain diametrically opposed to each other, suggesting another means of productively engaging the relationship between claims for community identity and inclusion from beyond the boundaries of that community (Nussbaum 1996, 6).

Taken together the chapters in this volume make the case that the logics of multiculturalism and the logics of foundationalism are not mutually exclusive. They are in fact complementary. As an issue of representation, claims asserting criteria for inclusion—whether in terms of multiculturalism or foundationalism—in some ways expand and in other ways contract citizenship identification. Broadly speaking, elaborations of shared representations of citizenship move in at least two directions at once, toward specificity of claims for recognition that appeal to difference and toward universality of claims for recognition that appeal to basic similarities shared by all persons. Representing citizenship as grounded in appeals to similarities, such as appeals to foundations or to cosmopolitan norms, attempt to anchor claims for community membership to the drawing of a common boundary for a community's concerns.

The intertwining of expansion and constraint with multiculturalism and foundational ideologies is the focus of this collection of essays. For ease of reference the first two chapters—one engaging founding ideologies by Rogers Smith, the other exploring multiculturalism by Will Kymlicka—are followed by five chapters that progressively elaborate these issues through analysis of representations of citizenship in differing times and places.

Nora Hui-Jung Kim, in "Political Activism 'of' or 'for' Migrants?" offers an analysis of a "retreat from multiculturalism," one led by immigrants who are supposed to benefit from such a philosophy, that critically enlarges Kymlicka's claim that appeals to multiculturalism still have merit. Despite the apparent retreat from multicultural rhetoric—a retreat that signals a "loss of confidence" in the multicultural—Kymlicka urges caution, pointing out that empirical data do not substantiate the failure of a multicultural agenda. Rather, the data available suggest to Kymlicka "cautious grounds for optimism" (XX). And so Kymlicka affirms that multicultural policies continue to serve indigenous peoples and minority national groups to a degree that precludes reversing course on multicultural policies.

Kim takes up such issues as they are experienced in South Korea. In 2010, South Korea received over 293,000 international migrants, a 70 percent rise over the number in 2000. As South Korea has become more diverse, multiculturalism has become more controversial, not least among the migrants themselves. They find themselves represented in policy debates by organizations designated by the central government to be their representatives, organizations that are well meaning but that frame their advocacy in ways that may undermine migrants' status. Kim's interviews with migrants show they are concerned that their representatives see them not as workers who deserve respect, but rather as people who deserve sympathy, thus perpetuating the "negative classification of migrants as less-than-full members of the Korean nation-state" (82).

In her contribution to this volume, "Triple Minorities Representing Majority Interests," Terri Susan Fine takes an approach similar to that of Kim, exploring the tensions between multiculturalism and democratic rule in terms of the dynamics of representation in government. Democratic bodies in the United States, including Congress and state legislatures, ordinarily operate on majoritarian principles. Election to a legislative seat is typically a two-person race, in which the majority vote-getter wins election. Within legislative bodies, however, it takes a majority or even a supermajority of delegate votes (such as the 60 percent of votes needed for cloture in the US Senate) to pass a bill. Between election and legislation, the representation of minorities is significantly diluted, so much so that Fine observes: "The majoritarian characteristics of electoral and legislative systems render it difficult for minorities to become integrated into US politics" (102). To demonstrate her point, Fine explores the dilemma of multiculturalism and democratic procedure by identifying the characteristics of Jewish female state legislators who, by virtue of their gender, religion, and sometimes party affiliation, occupy multiple minority statuses. Culling data from multiple sources, including state legislative directories, political almanacs, and news archives, Fine presents a snapshot of the individual and family characteristics, political experience, partisan affiliation, and states represented by Jewish female state legislators over a sixteen-year period, offering a basis for improving our understanding of how "minority groups succeed in majoritarian systems, and how citizenship is experienced through political representation in multi-cultural democracies" (107).

The chapters by Kim and Fine that explore appeals for inclusion and the institutionalization of exclusion are followed by John O'Keefe's chapter, "Alien Enemies or Naturalized Citizens?" O'Keefe describes the generation of the idea of British subjects as aliens in the United States as an outcome of early nineteenth-century efforts to define American citizenship. As O'Keefe argues, the Revolutionary War and the War of 1812 motivated legislation that narrowly defined American citizenship in relation to the exclusion of British subjects living in the United States, British subjects who in turn asserted broader, more ambivalent conceptions of citizenship. According to

O'Keefe the resistance of British subjects to exclusionary citizenship legislation made its impact on that legislation less through what those subjects claimed on their own behalf and more through the fact that those British subjects could appeal to shared culture, language, and ethnicity.

Kerry Wynn's contribution. "Civilizing the White Man," takes an approach resonant with that of O'Keefe, drawing our attention to another group of people—Native Americans living in Oklahoma—who share territory with European Americans who are claiming national identity as United States citizens. Wynn adds to considerations of how constructions of citizenship set the terms of inclusion and exclusion, demonstrating how Native Americans who were excluded from citizenship because they were seen as barbaric and uncivilized took upon themselves a discourse of hyper-civilization. By claiming their civilization superior to that of the United States, elite Oklahoma American Indians advocated for a correspondent superiority in their citizenship status. Wynn argues that such a strategy met with mixed results as it did not question the logic of associating civilization with citizenship. On the one hand, claims for rights that grounded in narratives of Native American civilization did provide empowering terms for claims to full United State citizenship. On the other hand, as progressive as those terms may have been, they did not prove progressive enough to counter the racialized hierarchies that drove rhetorics of civilizing.

"Museum-Making: 'New' Canadians Reimagine Heritage and Citizenship," Susan L. T. Ashley's contribution to this volume, argues that museums—while traditionally sites that reinforce the narrative of a nation's heritage—are also spaces within which citizens debate and discuss and so decide for themselves the place of those heritage narratives in their lives as citizens. Her two cases in point—the *Underground Railroad* exhibition at the Royal Ontario Museum and the Museo de la Solidaridad created by the Chilean community in Toronto—exemplify ways in which museums enlarge our senses of citizenship. While museum exhibits are static and some, such the *Underground Railroad* exhibition, are temporary, Ashley makes the case that those exhibits nonetheless do more than represent a heritage. Visitors to the exhibit must engage it and through that engagement take a more active role in their representations of their heritage as citizens. Ashley's example of the Museo de la Solidaridad further reflects citizens taking an active role in representing their citizenship through museum exhibitions. As Ashley explains, the Museo de la Solidaridad is an effort of Chilean immigrants in Toronto to build solidarity among Latin American citizens of Canada as well as to make a specifically Latin American contribution to Canadian citizenship. The ambitions for affirmation of a heritage and elaboration of a sense of citizenship through museum exhibitions cannot but confront boundaries of representing heritage and identity. But, as Ashley reminds us, it matters less having the last word and matters more continuing a dialogue out of the "positive knowledge-building and citizen-building connections that museum spaces and practices can offer" (168).

The understanding we can take away from this collection as a whole is that the means through which we represent and so establish the boundaries of our citizenship are never simple or straightforward. More than this we should take away the understanding that representations of citizenship ought never be so easily settled such that they become firmly established. In a globally connected environment, the grounding of citizenship in the geography of nations begins to lose hold as people are increasingly bound to each other across vast distances. The dual focus on multiculturalism and founding ideologies, as addressed by the essays in this volume, orient us to how representation figures in issues of citizenship: Representation is an important element of the process of "citizenization" (as Kymlicka defines it in his essay). Representation is an important component of the processes by which dominant groups accept the inclusion of subordinate groups in the national body, and representation is an important part of the process by which subordinate groups assert and gain membership in the national body. It is important to the mutually accepted accommodation of dominant and subordinate groups to each other. Finally, representation is vital not only to the process of accommodation, it is also central to the task of identifying the malleability of our deliberations and decisions as citizens. Ultimately, our very identities as citizens carry with them commitments and preferences and valuations that define/guide our membership in given communities that are themselves matters of representation.

WORKS CITED

Fraser, Nancy. 2003. "Social Justice in the Age of Identity Politics: Redistribution, Recognition, and Participation." In *Redistribution or Recognition? A Political Philosophical Exchange*, edited by Nancy Fraser and Axel Honneth. New York: Verso.

Markell, Patchen. 2003. *Bound by Recognition*. Princeton, NJ: Princeton University Press.

Nussbaum, Martha. 1996. "Patriotism and Cosmopolitanism." In *For Love of Country?*, edited by Martha Nussbaum and Joshua Cohen. Boston, MA: Beacon Press.

I

LINCOLN AND OBAMA

· · · · · · · · · ·

Two Visions of Civic Union

ROGERS M. SMITH

I'm left then with Lincoln, who like no man before or since understood both the deliberative function of our democracy and the limits of such deliberation. . . . It was a matter of maintaining within himself the balance between two contradictory ideas—that we must talk and reach for common understandings . . . and can never act with the certainty that God is on our side, and yet at times we must act nonetheless, as if we are certain. . . . Lincoln, and those buried at Gettysburg, remind us that we should pursue our own absolute truths only if we acknowledge that there may be a terrible price to pay.

Barack Obama, *The Audacity of Hope*

Barack Obama wrote the words above, invoking Abraham Lincoln as his political model, the year before he launched his presidential campaign at the Old State Capital in Springfield, Illinois, in 2007. Obama chose that spot to announce his candidacy because, as he explained, it is where Lincoln gave his "House Divided" speech in 1858, the address that began Lincoln's own rise to the White House. In his opening campaign speech, Obama referred to Lincoln repeatedly, ending with a sentence that echoed both Lincoln's Second Inaugural and the Gettysburg Address: "let us finish the work that needs to be done, and usher in a new birth of freedom on this Earth."[1] These invocations of Lincoln in writing, rhetoric, and symbolism were characteristic. From the time of his entry into national politics, Obama repeatedly identified himself with the first American president to emerge from Illinois.[2] It is not hard to see why Obama, seeking to be the first person of modern African descent elected to the presidency—indeed, the first such person elected leader of any predominantly European-descended nation anywhere in the world—would seek to link himself to the man who symbolizes the greatest instance of racial progress in US history, the end of African American slavery.

This essay canvasses parallels and contrasts in the careers and political visions of Lincoln and Obama, especially their views of the foundations and purposes of the American constitutional system and the forms of diversity that are and are not consistent with those foundations and purposes. The parallels are abundant, and although many of them are mere curiosities, one is significant indeed. Both men made the central theme of their initial presidential campaigns a particular conception of American civic union, of the ways the United States should and should not be diverse or, as we might say today, multicultural. Lincoln argued that American citizens should be devoted to realizing the principles of the Declaration of Independence and the forms of unity and diversity consistent with them. Obama contended that Americans should pursue the goal of "e pluribus unum" by constantly striving to discover and solve common problems and pursue common purposes without effacing legitimate differences.

But the similarities between Lincoln and Obama are accompanied by two fundamental contrasts. Lincoln's conception of civic union was a version of the natural rights republicanism that most nineteenth-century Americans embraced. Obama's understanding was a variant of the democratic pragmatist outlooks first elaborated in America's Progressive Era and eventually adopted by many but by no means all American leaders and citizens (Schulten 2009). And though it took time and unanticipated circumstances, Lincoln's vision of national union eventually generated a specific policy that he treated as an absolute and that served as the central guide and rallying point for his party: no slavery in the territories. Obama's vision did not generate and probably could not generate such a policy absolute. Instead, it produced a wide range of negotiated, compromise policy reforms, along with some controversial unilateral executive efforts to solve problems when negotiations failed. Although the two presidents' successes and failures resulted from many factors, their experiences shed light on the strengths and weaknesses of these two varieties of American public philosophy, especially in regard to the linked issues of philosophic foundations and multicultural diversity that remain central to citizenship and constitutional governance today.

PARALLEL LIVES

Although born elsewhere, Lincoln and Obama both moved to Illinois as young men and became lawyers. Both began their political careers in the Illinois state legislature, with Lincoln serving eight years in the Illinois House of Representatives from 1834 to 1842 (first elected at twenty-five) and Obama seven years in the Illinois Senate from 1997 to 2004 (first elected at thirty-six). Both men faced early setbacks: Lincoln was defeated in his first run for the Illinois House in 1832, Obama lost his bid for the US House in 2000. Both served briefly in Congress: Lincoln just over two years in the US House of Representatives, from December 1847 to March 1849; Obama nearly four years in the US Senate, from January 2005 to November 2008. Both men gained national stature as celebrated orators and as best-selling authors, Obama writing a memoir and a statement of political positions, Lincoln publishing the Lincoln-Douglas debate speeches. Both men had to defeat a more famous US senator from New York to win their party's nominations: William Seward in the case of Lincoln, Hillary Clinton in the case of Obama. Both then named their defeated rivals secretary of state.[3]

Of course, there are striking differences. Lincoln was virtually self-educated; Obama had an elite education at Occidental College, Columbia University, and Harvard Law School. Lincoln was a Republican, Obama a Democrat. Although many saw Lincoln as physically ugly, his persona was familiar and reassuring to most voters: a self-made white man whose name, Abraham Lincoln, invoked both the Christian religious and English ethnic roots with which so many Americans identified. Although many saw Obama as handsome, his persona was far less conventional, with an appearance most saw as black and a name, Barack Hussein Obama, that invoked Islamic and African roots. Still, no other presidents had such similar careers, including limited national legislative service and no executive experience, prior to becoming the nation's chief executive.

Of most concern here are their political principles, policies, and strategies. Despite their different parties, here too there are remarkable parallels. Most obvious is the identification of both men with racial progress. Less obvious is the criticism both men experienced for not going far enough on racial issues. In his second term in the Illinois legislature, Lincoln put himself on record as protesting the General Assembly's proslavery resolutions and as affirming "that the institution of slavery is founded on both injustice and bad policy," and that "the Congress of the United States has the power, under the Constitution, to abolish slavery in the District of Columbia" (Williams 1957, 4). In his term in Congress, Lincoln repeatedly voted for the Wilmot Proviso banning slavery in western territories, and he also drafted a bill to ban slavery in the District of Columbia, if its free inhabitants consented (Fredrickson 2008, 45). After the passage of the Kansas-Nebraska Act in 1854, which permitted those territories to adopt slavery, Lincoln made opposition to extending slavery his main issue, and it remained so through his election to the presidency in 1860 (Fredrickson 2008, 59–81).

But even as he condemned slavery in 1837, Lincoln also criticized "the promulgation of abolition doctrines" as something likely to "increase" slavery's "evils" (Williams 1957, 4). Up until 1863, he maintained that the national government had no power under the Constitution to ban slavery in states where it already existed and that it had a duty to return fugitive slaves to owners not in rebellion. He favored gradual emancipation, with compensation for slaveholders, and he regularly disavowed any desire for fully equal political and civil rights for African Americans, even as he insisted on their natural rights to the fruits of their labor (Fredrickson 2008, 59–113). Those urging instant universal emancipation and equal citizenship viewed these positions with contempt.

Barack Obama's early record on issues of race and civil rights is quickly summarized, but that fact also indicates why he faced criticism. After graduating from Harvard Law School in 1991, Obama returned to Chicago and directed Illinois's Project Vote, which succeeded in registering more than a third of the unregistered African Americans in the state. From 1993 to 2004, he worked with a law firm specializing in civil rights litigation and neighborhood economic development, and in those years he also taught constitutional law at the University of Chicago Law School, including civil rights cases. But apart from a bill to ban racial profiling by police, he was not identified with any substantial legislation on civil rights during his time in either the Illinois or the US Senate.[4] His rise to prominence symbolized progress for African Americans, but some thought he did not speak out strongly enough on racial issues (see Street 2010). Those criticisms only heightened during his presidency. Obama did not propose any major new racial policies and spoke about racial issues less than any president in over half a century, leaving most racial policy concerns to his attorney general, Eric Holder—though conservatives still accused Obama of caring only about black Americans, and views on previously nonracial issues like health care became racially skewed due to his association with them (Coates 2012).

Initially, Obama was instead most noted for a 2002 speech he gave against the looming Iraq war (Obama 2006, 47). He ran as the anti-Iraq war candidate, though Obama also contended that heightened efforts were needed against the Taliban in Afghanistan, and as president he authorized major increases in warfare there. Here, too, there is a parallel to Lincoln. Less than three weeks after taking his seat, freshman Representative Lincoln began introducing "spot resolutions" challenging the Polk administration's claims that Mexico had engaged in aggression on US soil, and he went on to attack the necessity and morality of the Mexican-American War (Lapsley 1906, 8: 103–7; Williams 1957, 25–33). Yet like Obama but to a far greater degree, Lincoln then became a militant wartime president. The difference here is that whereas Obama's stance on Iraq proved a political resource, Lincoln's opposition to the Mexican-American War was unpopular and led to his retreat to legal practice from 1849 to 1854.

Beyond issues of racial justice and war, there is another major parallel in the policies of Lincoln and Obama that Obama has repeatedly stressed. In *The Audacity of Hope*, Obama identified a tradition of "government investment in America's physical infrastructure and in its people" that began with Alexander Hamilton but that was "thoroughly embraced by Abraham Lincoln" and continued on through Theodore Roosevelt, Woodrow Wilson, and Franklin D. Roosevelt (Obama 2006, 152–53). Obama celebrated that tradition, saying that "we can be guided throughout by Lincoln's simple maxim: that we will do collectively, through our government, only those things we cannot do as well or at all individually and privately" (Obama 2006, 159). Obama was referring, as he would repeatedly, to a note Lincoln wrote in the summer of 1854, as he was reentering politics.[5] It read:

> The legitimate object of government, is to do for a community of people, whatever they need to have done, but cannot do, *at all*, or cannot, *so well do*, for themselves—in their separate, and individual, capacities. . . . The desirable things which the individuals

of a people cannot do or cannot well do, for themselves, fall into two classes. . . . The first—that in relation to wrongs—embraces all crimes, misdemeanors, and nonperformance of contracts. The other embraces all which, in its nature, requires combined action, as public roads and highways, public schools, charities, pauperism, orphanage, estates of the deceased, and the machinery of government itself. (Williams 1957, 38–39; italics original)

The position of both men—that government *is* entitled to do things that individuals cannot "*so well do*" for themselves—permits expansive governmental action whenever it is ambiguous whether individual or collective governmental action will be most effective. In practice both men as president quickly gave support to extensive new governmental programs. Although Lincoln ostensibly deferred to Congress on many domestic policy issues, there is no doubt that he favored what Daniel Elazar termed "Lincoln's New Deal." From 1861 through 1864, Congress created new national finance, revenue, and currency systems by establishing the Bureau of Internal Revenue and imposing the first income tax, along with sales and license taxes. It created paper "greenbacks" via the Legal Tender Act and a new Bureau of Printing and Engraving; imposed the high Morrill Tariff; and passed a series of National Banking Acts while creating a Comptroller of the Currency, as well as a money order system. It aided western settlement and development and the nation's transportation infrastructure via the creation of the Department of Agriculture, the 1862 Homestead Act, and a series of laws providing massive land grants to the railroads, and it also created the Yosemite nature reserve. It sought to provide fresh labor via the creation of an Office of Immigration and a Contract Labor Act in 1864. It provided for free urban mail delivery and a railway mail service. And it fostered education and research via the Morrill Land-Grant College Act and the creation of the National Academy of Science (Elazar 1965, 98–99; McPherson 1988, 443–53). It also created military pensions that became for a half century a kind of national welfare system (Skocpol 1992, 102–51). Although many of the financial measures were driven by the costs of war, these innovations collectively fit easily under the general headings of transportation, communications, and educational infrastructure and relief for those in need that Lincoln had listed in 1854, along with the support for banking and finance that had long been a Federalist and Whig staple and that Lincoln championed throughout his legislative career (Boritt 1978, 215–17). Not all these measures endured, but many did. They provided both national institutions and precedents for extensive federal aid, regulation, and even redistribution to spur and structure the nation's economic, educational, and technological development.

Obama's first two years in office, when he had Democratic majorities in both chambers, provided abundant evidence that, faced with the deepest economic recession since the Great Depression, the new president aggressively extended this "Hamilton-Lincoln-Roosevelts" tradition of national governmental action. He signed into law the Ledbetter Fair Pay Act, reauthorization of the Children's Health Insurance Program, legislation to help families avoid home mortgage defaults and to extend unemployment benefits, and a public lands management act designed to protect natural resources. He supported large loans and other forms of aid to financial institutions and to the automobile industry. His major economic measure, the American Recovery and Reinvestment Act of 2009, included stimulus funds and tax incentives for roads, bridges, mass transit, communications systems, wind and solar energy technologies and energy conservation, and jobs in health care, education, and state policing.[6] Then in March 2010, Obama signed the Patient Protection and Affordable Care Act, writing into law what he termed "the core principle that everybody should have some basic security when it comes to their health care" (Stolberg and Pear 2010). In July, he signed the Dodd-Frank Wall Street Reform Act, the most substantial changes in financial regulations since the New Deal.[7] In new forms, on a yet more massive scale, and with more pervasive regulatory and redistributive intent, these policy priorities tracked closely those Lincoln endorsed. And though the Republicans' capture of the House of Representatives in 2010 meant that Obama could not thereafter get major domestic initiatives through Congress, he often insisted the country needed to go further in these policy directions.

There is also another, less certain but perhaps deeper similarity in their thinking. The religious views of both men shifted from youthful skepticism to mature forms of faith that seem to involve substantial fatalism, combined with trust in an unknowable providence. Although Lincoln deplored religious zealotry and never belonged to a church, as the deaths for which he felt responsible mounted, his rhetoric became more religious, culminating in his second inaugural, which suggested that divine providence was at work in all that had happened, while admitting that he had no sure insight into divine plans (Fredrickson 2008, 52). Lincoln said of the warring sides:

Both read the same Bible, and pray to the same God; and each invokes His aid against the other. . . . The prayers of both could not be answered; that of neither has been answered fully. The Almighty has His own purposes. . . . Fondly do we hope—fervently do we pray—that this might scourge of war may speedily pass away. Yet if God wills that it continue, until all the wealth piled up by the bond-man's two hundred and fifty years of unrequited toil shall be sunk, and until every drop of blood drawn with the lash, shall be paid by another drawn with the sword, as was said three thousand years ago, so still it must be said, "the judgments of the Lord, are true and righteous altogether." (Williams 1957, 283)

These lines can be read as claiming divine justification for continuing the war to victory. Still, Lincoln insisted that "this terrible war" might be seen at best as "the woe due to those by whom the offense" of slavery came, both "North and South"—words that can also be read as accepting blame, not asserting righteousness (Williams 1957, 283).[8] Lincoln maintained, in Calvinistic fashion, that divine purposes are beyond human comprehension, and that though people must strive to do right, "as God gives us to see the right," their failings also mean that they must not expect their lives to be free from all-too-justified suffering.

Obama, raised by a skeptical, secular mother, found faith as a young man and used religious rhetoric throughout his career in national politics, often for inspirational purposes (Obama 2006, 202–8).[9] But he also often expressed a similar Calvinistic or Niebuhrian sensibility, notably when he accepted the Nobel Peace Prize even as he escalated American combat in Afghanistan. In Oslo he argued, "part of our challenge is reconciling two seemingly irreconcilable truths—that war is sometimes necessary, and war at some level is an expression of human folly."[10] Maintaining that "the one rule that lies at the heart of every major religion is that we do unto others as we would have them do unto us," Obama stated that adhering to this "law of love has always been the core struggle of human nature. For we are fallible. . . . Even those of us with the best of intentions will at times fail to right the wrongs before us. But we do not have to think that human nature is perfect for us to still believe that the human condition can be perfected." Citing Martin Luther King's Nobel Peace Prize acceptance speech, Obama urged that we "reach for the world that ought to be—that spark of the divine that still stirs within each of our souls." Acknowledging that "oppression will always be with us" and that "there will be war," it still made sense to "strive for justice" and to "strive for peace."[11]

In both men, this sense that human failings are ineradicable, so that terrible aspects of human experience will persist, but that it still makes sense to try to do right and pursue progress as much as possible, appears to have reinforced the general approach to politics for which Obama so often evoked Lincoln. That approach stresses pragmatic compromises, while still seeking to advance certain principles regarded as moral imperatives. In *The Audacity of Hope* Obama contended that Lincoln's "presidency was guided by a practicality that would distress us today, a practicality that led him to test various bargains with the South in order to maintain the Union without war; to appoint and discard general after general, strategy after strategy, once war broke out; to stretch the Constitution to the breaking point in order to see the war through to a successful conclusion" (Obama 2006, 97–98). And indeed, Lincoln indicated after his election that he would make concessions to the South to insure the return of fugitive slaves and to foreswear federal interference with the domestic slave trade and slavery in the District of Columbia (Ross 2009). In his first inaugural, he not only reiterated his denials that the federal government had power to restrict slavery in the states, he also added that he had no objection to a constitutional amendment irrevocably protecting slavery in existing states from federal interference (Williams 1957, 138–40, 146). Once in office, Lincoln offered compensation to slaveholders and programs of gradual emancipation and colonization long after these positions had been deemed unduly concessionary by many members of his party, much less abolitionists (Fredrickson 2008, 90–113).

Yet if Lincoln's approach to politics can justly be described as pragmatic and oriented toward compromise, that is not the whole story. As Obama recognized, Lincoln knew that "pragmatism can sometimes be moral cowardice" (Obama 2006, 98). More than many scholars have acknowledged, along with fierce ambition and calculated concessions, Lincoln's career also displayed a pattern of taking surprising political risks, from which he sometimes had to retreat. Lincoln suggested, perhaps but not plainly in jest, that women should have the right to vote on the same basis as men in 1836. And his denunciation of the injustice of slavery and assertion of congressional power to abolish slavery in the District of Columbia put him out in front of his Whig Party in 1837, as did his later condemnation of the Mexican-American War; the 1847 congressional bill against DC slavery he introduced; and his votes to ban slavery in the territories. He then refused to endorse Know-Nothing nativism at its height in the 1850s, and in 1857 he stated that not just black men but black *women* were entitled to Declaration of Independence rights (Williams 1957, 3; Lapsley 1906, 2: 20–22, 27–44, 246–99).

Most importantly, on the crucial issue of whether to offer the South the one concession that might have kept them in the Union in the winter of 1860/61—the establishment of slavery in the territories—Lincoln was unrelenting. He repeatedly told his allies that there was to be "no compromise on the question of *extending* slavery," and at Independence Hall on his way to his inauguration, Lincoln proclaimed that "if this country cannot be saved without giving up that principle . . . I would rather be assassinated on this spot than to surrender it" (Williams 1957, 133–34, 137; Ross 2009). In his final public speech on April 11, 1865, Lincoln said that in regard to enfranchising African Americans, his personal preference was for the vote to be "now conferred on the very intelligent, and on those who serve our cause as soldiers," thereby making at least some blacks full citizens (Lapsley 1906, 7: 366). That position proved risky indeed: John Wilkes Booth was in the audience and snarled, "That is the last speech he will ever make" (McPherson 1988, 852). The assassination Lincoln had imagined came three days later.

How does Obama's approach to politics compare to Lincoln's blend of pragmatism and principle, compromise making and risk taking? Although Obama often praised Lincoln's willingness to stand firm in the service of justice, he also repeatedly stressed that such conduct can have a "terrible price." In sharp contrast to Lincoln, Obama regularly contended that the Constitution rejects notions of "absolute truth" (Obama 2006, 93). Obama made clear both in word and deed his belief that the Constitution's system of popular self-governance involves political practices of "deliberative democracy" in which "all citizens are required to engage in a process of testing their ideas against an external reality, persuading others of their point of view, and building shifting alliances of consent" (Obama 2006, 92). In his own words, this view of democratic citizenship can "champion compromise, modesty, and muddling through; to justify logrolling, deal-making, self-interest, pork barrels, paralysis, and inefficiency" that "seem unprincipled" (94).

Obama always insisted, however, that such a politics of pragmatic consensus building can "also force groups to take other interests into account and, indeed, may even alter over time how those groups think and feel about their own interests," leading to "better, if not perfect, choices, not only about the means to our ends but also about the ends themselves." Those better choices can foster moral growth in the form of "new ideals, sharper visions, deeper values" (Obama 2006, 94–95). Perhaps in part because his sense of politics involved seeking to achieve such new and deeper moral insights, Obama, unlike Lincoln, never stated any "absolutes" on which he was "inflexible."

Yet even to assert that there are "better" choices about our ends and deeper values is to suggest that there are standards for judging what choices political leaders and voters ought to make, including what forms of diversity they should embrace and what forms they should reject. To discern Obama's standards, and to consider how they compare and contrast with Lincoln's, let us focus on what each presented as the core of his political vision: their conceptions of the character and aims of the American civic union.

LINCOLN'S CIVIC UNION: REALIZING THE PRINCIPLES OF THE DECLARATION

Many have suggested that during the course of his career, Lincoln showed allegiance to two values—the perpetuation of the American Union or nation, and principles of universal liberty that condemned slavery as wrong— though there are sharp disputes over which of these values took priority for him (Ross 2009; Fredrickson 2008, 1–41, 85). In 2008, George M. Fredrickson called attention to a third possibility, that of significant evolution in Lincoln's views over time. His analysis also calls attention to a third value: adherence to the American Constitution and the rule of law more generally—though Frederickson, like most scholars, treated that value as equivalent to support for the Union (Fredrickson 2008, 28, 50–53). Probably more than Fredrickson, I perceive substantial evolution in Lincoln's political vision from his days as a young Whig autodidact to his emergence as an architect and leader of the new Republican Party to his tragically aborted years presiding over the saving and then the initial reconstruction of America's constitutional system. Yet all three of these core elements—the commitments to union, constitutionalism, and to universal liberty—were there from the start. But as Dorothy Ross has noted, "linking universal principle to national identity" is both philosophically and politically problematic (Ross 2009, 385). That was all the more true in the United States, because the Constitution was commonly understood, and always understood by Lincoln, to provide some protections for slavery (Fredrickson 2008, 50).[12] The quest to realize principles of universal liberty, then, threatened both American constitutionalism and American union. Lincoln struggled first to acknowledge fully, then to address, those problems.

Lincoln said in his 1861 speech at Independence Hall that he had "never had a feeling politically that did not spring from the sentiments embodied in the Declaration of Independence," and there is no doubt he was sincere (Williams 1957, 137). But apart from his antislavery protest as a second-term state legislator and a brief passage in his 1842 speech to the Spring-field Washingtonian Temperance Society saying that the "revolution of '76" provided "the germ which . . . still is to grow and expand into the universal liberty of mankind," little in Lincoln's political career prior to his service in Congress suggested he gave any special emphasis to the Declaration (Lapsley 1906, 1: 161, 273). His chief themes were the value of internal improvements, banking, and education, and the need for adherence to enacted law over "mob law," including the lawlessness stirred by abolitionists (Lapsley 1906, 1: 123–28, 134–47, 151, 154, 196–228).

Even though in Congress he voted for the Wilmot Proviso and introduced his little-noticed bill to ban slavery in the District of Columbia, Lincoln said not long thereafter that he saw no way that slavery could be eradicated in the states where it was "deeply seated." He thought abolitionism threatened to "tear to tatters" the "venerated Constitution" and should be "execrated," so he endorsed the voluntary emancipation and transportation proposals of the American Colonization Society (Lapsley 1906, 2: 121–24, 169–74). As Lincoln later acknowledged, in these years, slavery was actually a "minor question" for him, apparently because he let himself believe, against all the evidence of slavery's entrenchment, that it was on a long, slow path to a peaceful death (Lapsley 1906, 3: 166; Fredrickson 2008, 43; Ross 2009).

When Lincoln relaunched his career by attacking Stephen Douglas's Kansas-Nebraska Act in 1854, he stated that the passage of that bill had "astounded" him, shattering this belief (Lapsley 1906, 2: 235). At Peoria, Illinois, that year, Lincoln explicitly fused his concerns for union, the Constitution and the rule of law, and principles of liberty into a common political vision, but he did so in ways he would soon modify. Lincoln argued for restoring the Missouri Compromise, meaning that Kansas and Nebraska should be admitted as free states. In so doing, he for the first time elaborated on the Declaration of Independence, finding in it "the leading principle, the sheet anchor of American republicanism"—but in 1854 he took that principle to be: "the just powers of government are derived from the consent of the governed" (Lapsley 1906, 2: 209; Schulten 2009, 810).

This was a risky assertion. Lincoln felt compelled to stress immediately that, despite the inescapable implication of that principle, he did not advocate "political," much less "social," equality for blacks and whites. Such equality, he had already said, felt intolerable to "the great mass of whites," whether or not their feelings accorded "with justice and sound judgment" (Lapsley 1906, 2: 191). Lincoln acknowledged that, far from embodying political equality, the Constitution favored slaveholders with added representatives, and though he called this "unfair," he disavowed any notion of altering or disregarding the Constitution (Lapsley 1906, 2: 214). He also asserted that as much as he hated slavery, he "would consent to the extension of it rather than see the Union dissolved" (216). But abandoning the Missouri Compromise was instead stirring "agitation" and "convulsions" that threatened a Union dependent on "the spirit of concession and compromise" (217, 219–20). Lincoln maintained that the framers had accepted only the argument of "necessity" in favor of slavery and "hemmed it in to the narrowest limits of necessity," and their policy should be restored (222–26).

At this point, then, Lincoln argued for respecting the Constitution and protecting slavery where it stood, but against its extension, on the grounds that it violated the Declaration's leading principle, the universal right of self-governance, and that extension endangered rather than aided the preservation of the Union. Still, the necessity of forging and maintaining the Union reconciled him to slavery's existence and its implicit constitutional protections, and he stated that such necessities might even reconcile him to slavery's extension, should saving the Constitution and the Union ever so require. This was a fusion of Constitution, union, and liberty that was far from satisfactory. It relegated liberty to a decidedly tertiary position. It thereby diminished the luster of the Constitution. And it rested all on strategies of compromise to maintain peace, with the claim that this strategy implied no slavery in Kansas or Nebraska, but little more.

But by 1856, Lincoln had cast his lot with the new Republican Party, a coalition of former Whigs and antislavery Democrats (many briefly members of Liberty and Free Soil parties) that found common ground on the principle of the Wilmot Proviso, "no slavery in the territories." Lincoln became a leader of the new party by elaborating this position, and in so doing he modified his larger views. In Springfield in 1857, Lincoln now presented the leading principle of the Declaration *not* as government by consent, but as equality in regard to the "inalienable rights" of "life, liberty, and the pursuit of happiness." He particularly stressed among these the antislavery, free labor right of every man and woman "to eat the bread she earns with her own hands" (Lapsley 1906, 2: 299–300).

This formulation sought to distance the Declaration's "leading principle" from the political rights of self-governance Lincoln had awkwardly endorsed, then partly disavowed, in 1854. Over time Lincoln would recognize that distance could not forever be sustained. But perhaps more significantly, Lincoln also now gave new prominence to the Declaration's liberties. They were not just the anchor of American republicanism; they defined the central goals that should guide the evolving policies of the American constitutional union, and all free governments, over time. The Declaration's authors, he said, "set up a standard maxim for free society" for "future use" which should be "constantly looked to, constantly labored for, and even though never perfectly attained, constantly approximated and thereby constantly spreading and deepening its influence and augmenting the happiness and value of life to all people, of all colors, everywhere" (Lapsley 1906, 2: 300–301).

In his "House Divided" speech and in the Lincoln-Douglas Senate debates the next year, Lincoln went further still toward a more steadfastly reformist view of constitutional union, in two regards. Although he was not yet prepared to argue that the protection of natural rights often required political rights, Lincoln now insisted that the old compromises could not be sustained forever, that "this government cannot endure half slave and half free." He indicated that the Republican policy of arresting the "further spread" of slavery was aimed at placing the institution "in the course of ultimate extinction" throughout the land (Lapsley 1906, 3: 2). Lincoln soon clarified that he fully accepted that "each community as a State has a right to do exactly as it pleases with all the concerns within that State that interfere with the right of no other State," so that each state could have its own distinct cranberry laws, oyster laws, or liquor laws (Lapsley 1906, 3: 52). But such diversity was not acceptable in regard to the "vast moral evil" of slavery: there, uniformity must be the ultimate goal (53). In the first Senate campaign debate, Lincoln added that he believed the framers, too, "intended and expected the ultimate extinction of that institution," and that he thought most of the public viewed it as rightly on the "course of ultimate extinction" prior to the Kansas-Nebraska Act (50, 65).

Although historically debatable, these claims about the framers' intentions and American public opinion, which Lincoln made often, allowed him to fuse his commitments to the Constitution and liberty more smoothly. The compromises of the Constitution were now understood as instruments not simply for the creation and preservation of the Union but for the gradual ending of slavery, in accordance with the goals defined by Declaration. Fidelity to the Constitution's purposes therefore required not permanent compromises but policies aimed at making the nation all free. The United States could and should remain diverse in many ways, with "variety" in the "industrial pursuits" appropriate to the "natural features" of their regions. But the nation must be on course to end the "vast moral evil" of slavery throughout the land, albeit in ways consistent with the Constitution and political practicality (Lapsley 1906, 3: 52–53; 4: 257–58, 263–65).

The vision of American civic union Lincoln painted in these speeches and thereafter—as devoted to finding peaceful, lawful ways to enable all Americans, and ultimately all humanity, to enjoy the basic natural rights announced in the Declaration of Independence, while permitting considerable diversity in all other regards—was not only more intellectually coherent, it also proved more politically compelling than his account in his 1854 speech. But it did not answer one great question. If policies putting slavery on the path to ultimate extinction, especially the Republicans' central principle, banning slavery in the territories, proved in fact to endanger the Union and the Constitution, should they nonetheless be pursued? The issue of Lincoln's answer to this question still divides scholars, with most contending that Lincoln always regarded saving the Union as more important than ever ending slavery (Fredrickson 2008, 85; Ross 2009).

Perhaps that judgment is correct. Against it stand three pieces of evidence. The first is Lincoln's correspondence to his allies as president-elect, in which he insisted that there be no compromise on the issue of extending slavery in the territories. The second is his 1861 speech in Philadelphia, where he portrayed the Union as kept together by "that sentiment in the Declaration of Independence which gave liberty, not alone to the people of this country, but, I hope, to the world for all future time . . . promise that in due time the weight would be lifted from the shoulders of all men" (Lapsley 1906, 5: 245). Lincoln asked, "can the country be saved upon that basis?" and said if it could not, "it will be truly awful"—and it was then that he said he would rather be assassinated than "surrender" that basis of union (245). This statement confirmed that he had come to reject his 1854 view accepting the extension of slavery if necessary to save the union. Now Lincoln contended that it was morally unacceptable and politically impossible to preserve the union without agreement on the aim of realizing the Declaration's principles. The final piece of evidence for this fixed commitment is Lincoln's deeds: when faced a few months later with the actual choice of whether to accept war with the seceding South or instead offer them the concession of universal slavery to bring them back in the union, Lincoln chose war.

Perhaps Lincoln had no other option. His new party and his campaign had been built on the policy plank of no slavery in the territories. Lincoln might well have thought he would lose all support if he backed away from the position with which he was most identified. To point to loss of support alone, however, is not to prove that Lincoln had no alternative. It might only suggest that he valued his own power more than saving the union. There can be no doubt that Lincoln was an ambitious man, intimately familiar with the soul that "thirsts and burns for distinction" (Lapsley 1906, 1: 158). More charitably, Lincoln might have believed that offering that great concession simply would not work, that the South or antislavery forces would reject his attempt, and war would still come.

But it is more likely that Lincoln now genuinely saw any acceptance of slavery in the territories as immoral. It was Lincoln himself who took the lead in rejecting any talk of such a compromise. It was also Lincoln who went on, as Obama noted, to bend if not break his revered Constitution in his efforts to win the war, and who by its end came to support universal, immediate, uncompensated emancipation via the Thirteenth Amendment and to encourage states to adopt at least a limited franchise for African American men, positions he had previously rejected. It is therefore reasonable to interpret the mature Lincoln's political vision in the way that Obama has done: as placing very high value on both constitutionalism and union and as embracing a pragmatic politics of compromises and concessions—but only insofar as they can be seen, on balance and over time, to be contributing to realizing the commitments of the Declaration of Independence, that all humanity should enjoy the basic liberties of life, liberty, and the pursuit of happiness, including rights of free labor. According to this understanding, it was necessary to take very great risks and to pay a terrible price to insure that the Constitution and union were saved only "on that basis."

OBAMA'S CIVIC UNION: PURSUING THE ELUSIVE PROMISE OF "E PLURIBUS UNUM"

If it is right to suggest that Lincoln's views shifted from 1855 to 1865, aided by the pressures and opportunities that came from finding a central issue—no slavery in the territories—that led him to give greater coherence to his vision of American union, Barack Obama showed little similar development until, at most, his second term. Up to then, his writings, speeches, policy decisions, and his political strategies all remained consistent with the themes he laid out in his breakthrough 2004 Democratic Convention address, even though changing circumstances led him to different emphases at different times.

Those themes have always stressed the need to find compromise solutions to a range of common problems, including economic growth and aid to the needy, education, health care, energy, the environment, transportation, and more. Although many now see the Affordable Care Act as Obama's signature issue, he did not make health care reform the focus of his 2008 campaign. Obama did make it an early priority, and he then had to defend "Obamacare" repeatedly against a passionate countermobilization and legal challenges. But unlike Lincoln's opposition to the expansion of slavery, Obama never framed health care as the preeminent imperative his constitutional philosophy demanded. Throughout his career, Obama's central message was not any one policy, but rather his democratic pragmatist vision of cooperative, deliberative, problem-solving politics, accompanied by a moderately expressed endorsement of social justice goals (Smith 2012).

The striking irony that emerges from comparing the two men's constitutional visions and broader worldviews is that Lincoln's assertion of an unchanging moral absolute, derived from a foundation of natural rights, contributed to his evolution on a range of policies, particularly political rights for African Americans. As the war proceeded, he also relied more heavily on religious rhetoric to convey his sense of the nation's unalterable moral goals. In contrast, Obama's proudly flexible foundational pragmatism generated fewer policy changes during his presidency, nor until late in his presidency did he come to articulate more prominently his black church-inspired social justice understanding of Americans' shared purposes.

He did so most stirringly in his eulogy for the victims of the Charleston, South Carolina, church shooting on June 26, 2015. There, invoking the deep involvement of black churches in America's struggles for civil rights, Obama maintained in clear social gospel terms that "our Christian faith demands deeds and not just words," and deeds aimed at not just "individual salvation" but the "collective salvation" that includes feeding the hungry, clothing the naked, housing the homeless, and pursuing the "steady expansion of human rights and human dignity in this country; a foundation stone for liberty and justice for all."[13] Obama referred to a number of public policies that might further these aims. He also, however, stressed that "collective salvation" required "more than any particular policy," an "open heart," a "reservoir of goodness," found through "amazing grace."[14] Although his religiously justi-fied sense of social justice purposes was more conspicuous than ever before, his reluctance to assert policy absolutes remained. In terms of policy, the chief shift in Obama's conduct, especially after further Democratic defeats in 2014, was to bow to the nation's still-intensifying polarization by muting his long-standing countertheme of "e pluribus unum" and his faith in deliberative democratic processes. Instead, he relied increasingly on unilateral executive acts for immigration, criminal justice, housing, education, and other reforms that were both controversial and yet, given the legal and political barriers to such measures, necessarily limited in scope (Korte 2014b).

This shift to executive unilateralism did not come easily, for Obama always certified the feasibility of deliberative collective problem solv-ing despite differences through his own life story. In his 2004 speech he expressed his gratitude "for the diversity of my heritage," even as he stressed that his biography was "part of the larger American story" in ways that made him indebted to America, since "in no other country on earth" could his story be "even possible."[15] Like Lincoln, Obama then traced that possibility to America's commitment to the principles of the Declaration of Inde-pendence, and he argued that, "with just a slight change" in public policies, Americans could "make sure that every child in America has a decent shot at life, and that the doors of opportunity remain open to all." Then Obama went on to elaborate the case for governmental action in his signature fashion, arguing that "alongside our famous individualism, there's another ingredient in the American saga, a belief that we're all connected as one people. . . . I am my brother's keeper, I am my sister's keeper. . . . It's what allows us to pursue our individual dreams and yet still come together as one American family. E pluribus unum: 'Out of many, one.'"[16]

The larger story of American civic union that Obama portrayed, then, was one that still took the "standard maxim" of the Declaration of Independence as its guide, but it stressed, using familial and biblical language, obligations for Americans to work together to assist one another. Obama portrayed those duties as responsibilities of citizenship deriving from shared debts to American predecessors as well as from Americans' contemporary connectedness. As his Charleston eulogy confirmed, this sense of shared civic responsibilities has remained a constant in Obama's rhetoric, from his 2007 announcement speech, where he said his campaign was "about reclaiming the meaning of citizenship, restoring our sense of common purpose";[17] to his first inaugural address, in which he insisted "we have duties to ourselves, our nation, and the world. . . . This is the price and promise of citizenship";[18] to his 2012 nomination acceptance speech, where he maintained that Americans' beliefs in inalienable rights fostered commitments to "personal responsibility" and "individual initiative," but also to "citizenship . . . the idea that this country only works when we accept certain obligations to one another and to future generations";[19] and to his second inaugural, where Obama called the Declaration's self-evident truths of human equality and inalienable rights "what makes us Americans," while insisting that "preserving our individual freedoms ultimately requires collective action . . . as one nation and one people . . . as citizens."[20]

But just as Lincoln faced tensions in trying to affirm both constitutional union and universal liberty, Obama's insistence that Americans could pursue their diverse "individual dreams" and still "come together" through democratic processes of deliberation and compromise to meet their challenges as "one people" has always faced problems. How can a country that embraces diversity be sure that *all* will find their individual dreams and liberty fulfilled in the conceptions of common purposes that emerge from pragmatic democratic politics? Obama's hope has been that by linking the goals of the Declaration with commitments to mutual assistance, America's common purposes will consist precisely in people helping each other to exercise their preferred forms of liberty and pursuits of happiness. For Obama, American diversity is premised on, not a basis for arguing against, recognizing the rights of the Declaration of Independence for all—in exactly the same way that, as Will

Kymlicka argues in this volume, most modern multiculturalists derive their values and policies from commitments to human rights.

Yet just as there are controversies over when and which human rights trump multicultural claims, and over whether multiculturalism is too fragmenting, Obama's hopes for harmonizing embrace of many forms of diversity with expanding rights for all often ran into political trouble. Many Americans did not accept that their pursuits of happiness entailed the responsibilities to others Obama depicted. Others felt they could not compromise when Obama's "common goals" threatened their religious and cultural traditions, or when the distinctive lifestyles of others seemed to violate the common purposes they thought most crucial. Whenever such moral differences are widespread and deeply felt, they make it very hard to achieve "e pluribus unum" policies through deliberative democratic procedures.

Obama himself highlighted the limitations of democratic proceduralism in regard to the moral issue central to Lincoln. When it came to slavery, Obama wrote in 2006, America's democratic "conversation" broke down, because "deliberation alone could not provide the slave his freedom or cleanse America of its original sin. In the end, it was the sword that would sever his chains" (Obama 2006, 92, 94–96). But Obama was hopeful that democratic processes could now address racial controversies more successfully than in Lincoln's day, because "reformers" had since employed American "ideals of equality" to form "a multicultural nation the like of which exists nowhere else on earth" (232, 243). This diversity created new opportunities for coalition building and compromises, so that unlike Lincoln, Obama saw no need to define moral absolutes on civil rights issues, any more than on others.

To be sure, Obama still often advanced "a word of caution" about whether "we have arrived at a 'postracial' politics" or "already live in a color-blind society" (Obama 2006, 232). Noting the stark statistics on persisting racial inequalities and his own experiences of racism, he sometimes raised today's central racial dispute: whether policies should be strictly color blind, enacted without racial classifications or a focus on racial consequences, or race conscious, continually assessed to see whether policies are diminishing or exacerbating racial inequalities, in ways that might support race-targeted programs. Most Americans, particularly white Americans, favor color-blind policies. Obama's core constituents, white liberals and nonwhites, favor race-conscious measures (see, e.g., King and Smith 2011).

Predictably, on this battleground issue, Obama always trod carefully. On the one hand he maintained that affirmative action, "when properly structured, can open up opportunities otherwise closed to qualified minorities without diminishing opportunities for white students," and that "where there's strong evidence of prolonged and systematic discrimination by large corporations, trade unions, or branches of municipal government, goals and timetables for minority hiring may be the only meaningful remedy available" (Obama 2006, 244). But, conveying his empathy with those who favor color-blind measures, Obama also urged an "emphasis on universal, as opposed to race-specific programs" as both "good policy" and "good politics" (247). He held that "proposals that solely benefit minorities and dissect Americans into 'us' and 'them' may generate a few short-term concessions when the costs to whites aren't too high, but they can't serve as the basis for the kinds of sustained, broad-based political coalitions needed to transform America" (248).

Even on racial issues, then, Obama sought to lead Americans to find common ground, joining those who favor color-blind policies, but who do want to see real material racial progress and can tolerate a few race-conscious measures, with those who think substantial race-conscious measures are needed, but who are willing to see them put on the back burner if progress is being achieved through other means. And unlike Lincoln, both as a candidate and later as president, Obama pursued this strategy simply by talking very little about race, permitting color-blind and race-conscious advocates to interpret his rhetorical emphases on unity and change in terms congenial to them.

Indeed, after he began pursuing the presidency actively, Obama only spoke on race at length once, when forced to do so by the controversy over his pastor, the Reverend Jeremiah Wright, in March 2008. Obama began by interpreting the Constitution like Lincoln: as "stained by this nation's original sin of slavery," but with "the answer to the slavery question" already "embedded" in it, because the "Constitution . . . had at its very core the ideal of equal citizenship under the law" and "promised its people liberty, and justice, and a union that could be and should be perfected over time." Obama then portrayed US history as a "long march for a more just, more equal, more free, more caring and more prosperous America." To continue, Obama asserted, Americans needed to see "that we may have different stories, but we hold common hopes . . . we all want to move in the same direction," defined by "the idea that . . . out of many, we are truly one."[21]

Obama then contended that the nation's racial disparities could often "be directly traced to inequalities passed on from an earlier generation that suffered under the brutal legacy of slavery and Jim Crow." But Obama counseled against labeling "the resentments of white Americans" over affirmative action and their "fears of crime" as "misguided or even racist." Instead, Obama urged "the African-American community" to bind "our particular grievances" to "the larger aspirations of all Americans," including "the white woman struggling to break the glass ceiling, the white man who's been laid off, the immigrant trying to feed his family." Obama then advised the "white community" that "the path to a more perfect union means acknowledging that ... the legacy of discrimination—and current incidents of discrimination, while less overt than in the past—are real and must be addressed" with "deeds." Those deeds were the tasks of government that Lincoln defined: "investing in our schools and our communities ... enforcing our civil rights laws and ensuring fairness in our criminal justice system ... providing this generation with ladders of opportunity that were unavailable to previous generations." Obama urged "all Americans to realize ... that investing in the health, welfare and education of black and brown and white children will ultimately help all of America prosper."[22]

In so arguing, Obama foreshadowed how his administration would not define any clear and overt, much less uncompromising, approach to racial inequalities. Instead, it would neither wholly repudiate nor emphasize race-conscious measures, while continuing to stress "universal" programs. Those programs often would quietly be selected because of their potential to close racial gaps, so that public policies would in fact be evaluated on race-sensitive grounds. But assisting all Americans, not any particular group, would be their avowed (and genuine) aim. In this way Obama suggested that, unlike the time of slavery, today even the profound grievances of African Americans could best be addressed by discerning how they were served by evolving common goals, rather than by committing to any policies presented as fixed moral absolutes.

OBAMA'S VISION OF CIVIC UNION IN AN ERA OF POLARIZATION

Although almost unique in its explicit exploration of race, Obama's 2008 speech was of a piece with what he had said before and what he would go on to say and do on all issues. Unlike Lincoln, Obama consistently stressed that *all* policies should be seen as evolving experimental solutions to changing problems, needs, and popular desires, ideally derived from the ideas of both parties and adopted via extensive congressional as well as executive deliberation. In his first term, commentators who failed to grasp this philosophy expressed surprise at Obama's "deference to Congress," noting that the "stimulus package was largely written by members of the Appropriations committees, with concessions made to . . . three Republicans," while the health care bill, which used insurance concepts pioneered by the Heritage Foundation, was also at first labored on chiefly by congressional leaders including Republican senator Charles Grassley (Barone 2009). Critics contended that Obama was relying too much on Congress, and in the end he and his allies found they could enact the bill only over fierce, unanimous Republican opposition (including Grassley) (see, e.g., Robinson 2010; Packer 2010, 40–51). But even as Obama called providing "some" health security a "core principle," he praised the Affordable Care Act (ACA) not as an acknowledgment of any fixed moral absolute but only an expression of "that essential truth, a truth every generation is called to rediscover for itself, that we are not a nation that scales back its aspirations" (Stolberg and Pear 2010). His emphasis remained on democratic quests to find broadly acceptable policies.

This constitutional vision, far more akin to John Dewey than to John Locke, has long drawn criticisms from conservatives for manifesting a modern philosophic relativism that represents to them a disturbing declension from Lincoln's insistence that the nation take guidance from "moral and abstract right" whenever possible (Lapsley 1906, 4: 116; Schulten 2009, 817). Obama's philosophy has also been faulted as less suited to building enduring coalitions committed to justice than more absolutist views. At this writing, less than two years before the end of Obama's second term, it is reasonable to consider what Obama's record suggests about the strengths and limits of his conception of America's civic union in comparison to Lincoln's, and about the broader worldviews of modern democratic pragmatism and older natural rights republicanism that their linked yet contrasting views express. Although Obama can claim more accomplishments than many critics concede, his decision to favor pragmatism over the pursuit of clear moral purposes failed to moderate the nation's combustible political polarization. Instead, many of Obama's hopes were consumed by the flames of ideological intransigence.

Nonetheless, in many ways the parallels in their political lives followed the two men through their presidencies. Like Lincoln, Obama began with his party in control of both chambers of Congress and the White House. Obama's circumstances were in fact more favorable: his Democrats won major victories in the 2008 election, while Lincoln's Republicans controlled Congress only because many southern Democrats left to join their seceding states. Both presidents then quickly oversaw the passage of many laws that were historic in substance and magnitude—but Lincoln's presidency was dominated by the unexpectedly costly war he pursued, while Obama's was dominated by a slow if steady economic recovery and unanticipated outrage over what became, in the end, his signature health care law. The parties of both men suffered major losses in the midterm elections of their first terms, though in 1862 Lincoln's Republicans retained control of both chambers, while in 2010 Obama's Democrats lost the House. Yet despite periods of severe unpopularity in their first terms, both presidents were reelected by comfortable margins. Lincoln was killed barely a month after his second inauguration, while Obama struggled against often fatal opposition in the House to most of his second-term policies.

Lincoln's success in winning the war and ending slavery meant that his pragmatic politics in pursuit of what he took to be the moral absolute of putting slavery on the path to extinction has come to be widely venerated as the nation's greatest presidency—not least by Barack Obama. Today it is likely that many will view Obama's presidency as having relatively few major achievements after the first two years. Sympathetic commentators have credited him with preventing the 2008 recession from turning into a Depression and with fulfilling the Democrats' six-decade-old goal of creating national health insurance, among other accomplishments (Glastris 2012). Defenders have also noted that, although Obama often spoke of the middle class and universal programs rather than the poor or racial minorities, during his first term his proposals for means-tested spending programs, as well as governmental expenditures to aid the poor, greatly exceeded those of most of his predecessors, including Democrats Bill Clinton and Jimmy Carter (Mendelberg and Butler 2014, A23).

But not only did his first administration spur the Tea Party insurgency in the Republican Party that led to gridlock in national lawmaking, Obama also received increasingly sharp criticism from many former supporters for failing to address, much less reduce, racial inequalities, for extensive deportations of unauthorized immigrants, and for severe national security measures, including drones for targeted assassinations abroad and electronic surveillance at home (Hickey 2014; Law 2014).[23] Because so much of Obama's promise was associated with progress on civil rights, and because it is the arena where the contrast between Lincoln's natural rights liberalism and Obama's more pervasive democratic pragmatism is sharpest, it is appropriate to give particular attention to his record there in assessing the strengths and limits of his approach to civic governance.

It is first clear that Obama's strategy of stressing color-blind or universalist approaches to American inequalities without rejecting all race-conscious policies failed to build consensus on many issues. Despite Obama's lack of racial rhetoric, conservative commentators including Glenn Beck and Rush Limbaugh regularly accused him of being a "racist" or "reverse racist."[24] He was also buffeted by controversies over the race-conscious remarks of his Supreme Court nominee, Sonia Sotomayor, who suggested that at times a "wise Latina" might be able to reach better decisions than a white man (Bash and Sherman 2009). In his second term, Obama did publicly champion a modest race-conscious program that drew its title from his favorite religious imagery—the "My Brother's Keeper" initiative in which a mix of public and largely private sources were to contribute $200 million over five years to assist young men of color to obtain education and employment. Conservatives denounced it, too, as racist (Remnick 2014).

Because Obama generally chose to defend his racial policies in courtrooms rather than electoral contests, attorney general Eric Holder served as the administration's "leading voice on racial issues," but as a result, Holder was held in contempt of Congress by House conservatives and denounced as "the most divisive Attorney General in modern history" (Korte 2014a). And as Obama's Justice Department strove to maintain a measure of race-consciousness in national policies, it suffered some major judicial defeats. In *Ricci v. DeStefano* (2009), the Supreme Court ruled that a city fire department could not use racial considerations as a basis even for moving from one type of facially race-neutral test to another.[25] Public policies had to be more fully color blind, even if racial inequalities persisted as a result. In *Shelby County v. Holder* (2013), the Court invalidated Section 4 of the Voting Rights Act of 1965 and its formula requiring preclearance for states that had low voter registration or turnout rates in 1964, rules that Justice Scalia disparaged as "perpetuation of racial entitlement" (Weiss 2013). And in *Schuette v.*

Coalition to Defend Affirmative Action (2014), the Court upheld Michigan's ban on affirmative action in higher education, over a passionate dissent from Justice Sotomayor, who feared the end of needed "race sensitive" policies (Liptak 2014). Obama's decision to leave advocacy of race-conscious policies to his attorney general appeared unable to win political benefits or to preserve many race-conscious measures, and even supporters conceded his administration saw few significant gains, and some losses, for African Americans. It was therefore far from clear that his pragmatic compromises on racial issues were truly providing consensual solutions that advanced social justice objectives.

Similarly, Obama struggled to overcome a variety of other "diversity" challenges to his constitutional vision of e pluribus unum. Catholic institutions, corporations owned by religious believers, and other nonprofits challenged the Affordable Care Act's requirements that they at least indirectly aid their employees to obtain insurance plans that covered contraceptives, for they saw these rules as burdens on their religious freedom (National Women's Law Center 2014). The Supreme Court decided against the administration in *Burwell v. Hobby Lobby Stores* (2014), in an opinion written so broadly that it invited many more lawsuits against federal measures on religious grounds (Liptak 2014). The controversies dramatized the issue of whether in the multicultural America of the twenty-first century it was possible to give policy content to the putative common goals of Americans without appearing to fail to accommodate adequately the great diversity of moral values Americans in fact exhibited.

Those difficulties were reinforced by the challenges Obama experienced in foreign affairs. Again like Lincoln, who hoped that the aims of the Declaration of Independence would eventually extend to "the world for all future time," Obama repeatedly indicated that his vision of the goals of America's civic union applied to all humanity (Lapsley 1906, 2: 299–300; 5: 245). In a speech at Cairo in 2009, Obama restated his claim that America was "shaped by every culture, drawn from every end of the Earth, and dedicated to a simple concept: E pluribus unum—'Out of many, one.'" Unity was possible despite such diversity because "regardless of race, religion, or station in life, all of us share common aspirations—to live in peace and security; to get an education and to work with dignity; to love our families, our communities, and our God. . . . This is the hope of humanity." Globally as domestically, Obama argued that all people "have a "responsibility . . . to one another as human beings" to work together to fulfill this hope. And he said that though his "first duty as President" was "to protect the American people," the world's "interdependence" meant that "any world order that elevates one nation or group of people over another will inevitably fail." All leaders must "use diplomacy and build international consensus to resolve our problems whenever possible."[26]

This view meant that Obama generally sought to rely on multilateral solutions to international problems in ways that respected international diversity. He argued that each nation "gives life" to principles of democracy and human rights "in its own way, grounded in the traditions of its own people," and he characteristically called for all not to focus on "what pushes us apart," but to commit to "a sustained effort—to find common ground, to focus on the future we seek for our children, and to respect the dignity of all human beings."[27] As his nuclear power agreement with Iran later showed, Obama was willing to work even with the nation's most hostile enemies in this quest.

But as foreign policy crises unfolded, Obama often decided that national security concerns compelled him to use unilateral coercive sanctions and military force in order to protect the American people against threats from Iran, from Islamic militants in Afghanistan, Pakistan, Iraq, and Syria, and elsewhere. He also contended he had to act in ways that bent if they did not break constitutional restrictions, ordering killings abroad of American citizens and supporting pervasive covert surveillance operations domestically and internationally. And as he came to doubt the capacity of a polarized Congress to act, Obama increasingly claimed that he could pursue national security measures strictly on his own executive authority, without congressional approval (Cole 2012; Granick and Sprigman 2013; Healy 2014).

These actions showed that Obama's belief in deliberative democracy and his faith in multilateralism were far from self-evident truths, even for him. Yet among the international leaders and movements with whom he sought to forge alliances, as with his domestic critics on the right and the left, there were many who saw Obama's willingness to rely on unilateral actions as arrogant, undemocratic, and unconstitutional. Obama's vision required him to walk a tightrope between his more hawkish domestic critics who saw his conception of Americanism as far too open to surrenders of national sovereignty, and those at home and abroad who saw it as a stance that refused to accept that the era of sovereign nation-states, much less the United States as the hegemonic nation-state, was and ought to be coming to an end.

The evidence suggests that Obama's constitutional vision of achieving unity without effacing diversity via deliberative democratic politics, all in the service of realizing the promises of the Declaration of Independence, did not succeed in diminishing polarizing trends and forming a more perfect union. Instead, his confidence in deliberative democracy at home and abroad seemed to weaken. During his reelection campaign in 2012, Obama said that "the mistake of my first term" was "thinking that this job was just about getting the policy right . . . the nature of this office is to tell a story to the American people that gives them a sense of unity and purpose and optimism, especially during tough times" (Boerma 2012). But his campaign website replaced its 2008 assertion that Obama's diverse background would enable him to "unite people around a politics of purpose" with the simple contention that he was "driven by the same values that make our country great: America prospers when we're all in it together."[28] The change suggested Obama still believed all Americans should unite, but he no longer felt able to claim he was the person who could convince them of that. In his 2016 State of the Union address, Obama concluded that one of the "few regrets" of his presidency was that, rather than realizing the goal of e pluribus unum, "rancor and suspicion between the parties has gotten worse instead of better" (Obama 2016).

In his second inaugural address, Obama did return to his central themes in a way that invoked American social justice traditions more boldly, saying "the most evident of truths—that all of us are created equal—is the star that guides us still; just as it guided our forebears through Seneca Falls and Selma and Stonewall; just as it guided all those men and women, sung and unsung, who left footprints along this great Mall, to hear a preacher say that we cannot walk alone; to hear a King proclaim that our individual freedom is inextricably bound to the freedom of every soul on Earth" (Obama 2013). Obama thereby connected his civic vision more overtly to women's rights and GLBT rights, as well as to black church-led struggles for African American civil rights. But after this speech, Obama rarely pressed his claim that the nation's central purpose was the goal of making "values of life and liberty and the pursuit of happiness real" for all, with continuing civil rights reforms the milestones of progress. Instead, Obama often simply noted, most eloquently in Charleston, that for him American values were rooted in religious social justice traditions. He remained cautious about presenting his principles as moral absolutes that, even more than democratic processes, should define American aims. And so the possibility arises: perhaps if Obama, like Lincoln, had insisted more firmly on the moral rightness of his constitutional vision, he might not have been able to claim so great a commitment to unity or deliberative democracy—but he might in the end have done still more to realize what he believed to be the highest goals of constitutional self-governance.

CONCLUSION

The comparison of Lincoln's and Obama's conceptions of civic union may seem to favor Lincoln's nineteenth-century natural rights liberalism over Obama's modern democratic pragmatism, and Lincoln's insistence on certain moral absolutes over Obama's hopes for consensual, deliberative, evolving multiculturalism. And however history may judge Obama, Lincoln will surely always loom far larger.

Yet it must also be said, not only that Obama had achievements that deserve to be ranked as historic, whether one approves of them or not, but that his efforts were often frustrated by his genuinely deep commitment to addressing differences democratically, instead of responding to severe polarization, as Lincoln did, with force. However we judge the rectitude of Lincoln's refusal to compromise on what he saw as a moral absolute, Obama was surely right to stress in the passage cited at the start of this chapter that the nation paid a terrible price for this refusal. Few of Obama's critics would have preferred for him to accomplish more by asserting executive powers and bursting constitutional boundaries even further than he did. Most would agree that as inefficacious as democratic processes often are, most, perhaps all, alternative forms of governing are worse. Obama's more thoroughly democratic pragmatic vision may simply have been less suited to the challenges of his time than Lincoln's.

With that said on Obama's behalf, it is still significant that Lincoln's career displayed more growth in his understanding of what his own vision required of him and the nation than Obama's. And Lincoln responded to adversity by making clearer to all Americans, including himself, what the commitments of America's core principles, as he understood them, required of the nation. When faced with mounting political antagonisms, Obama's efforts to articulate why Americans should have "a sense of unity and purpose" and to define the policies fulfilling those purposes often faltered. Those who seek to build on Obama's legacy must therefore consider whether, even if they do not feel they can assert "abstract right" with the certainty of Enlightenment rationalists or Social Gospel believers, they do need to recognize that inclusive democratic unity may not always be the nation's highest goal, and that leaders must sometimes try to speak, not primarily to Americans as they are, but to the better angels of their nature, if their nation is to be stirred to pursue forms of civic union more perfect than those achieved so far.

NOTES

1. "Barack Obama's Opening Campaign Speech," www.guardian.co.uk/world/2007/feb/10/barackobama, accessed March 5, 2010.

2. In the 2004 Democratic Convention keynote address that won him national fame, Obama introduced himself as from the "Land of Lincoln." Accessed March 5, 2010, at www.americanrhetoric.com/speeches/convention2004/barackobama2004dnc.htm. Ulysses Grant, the only other president to run from Illinois, moved to the state in 1860 and was not involved in politics before winning fame during the Civil War.

3. Harold Holzer, "The Real Ties between Lincoln and Obama," www.cnn.com/2009/POLITICS/01/16/holzer.lincoln.obama/, accessed March 5, 2010; "Abraham Lincoln Political Career Timeline," http://showcase.netins.net/web/creative/lincoln/education/polbrief.htm, accessed March 5, 2010; "Barack Obama," http://en.wikipedia.org/wiki/Barack_Obama, accessed March 5, 2010.

4. "Barack Obama," http://en.wikipedia.org/wiki/Barack_Obama, accessed March 5, 2010.

5. Obama invoked this passage without citation in his "Closing Statement" on October 27, 2008, and discussed it in his "Lincoln 200th Birthday Speech" on February 12, 2009. See http://blogs.suntimes.com/sweet/2008/10/obama_closing_argument_speech_1.html; www.buzzflash.com/articles/node/7708, both accessed March 5, 2010.

6. "Barack Obama," http://en.wikipedia.org/wiki/Barack_Obama, accessed March 5, 2010.

7. www.gpo.gov/fdsys/pkg/PLAW-111publ203/html/PLAW-111publ203.htm, accessed August 18, 2015.

8. In his December 1, 1862, "Annual Message to Congress," Lincoln had written, "the people of the South are not more responsible for the original introduction" of slavery than "the people of the North; and when it is remembered how unhesitatingly we all use cotton and sugar and share the profits of dealing in them, it may not be quite safe to say that the South has been more responsible than the North for its continuance" (Lapsley 1906, 6: 201).

9. In his 2004 Democratic nominating speech, Obama asserted, "We worship an awesome God in the Blue States," and argued that "God's greatest

gift to us, the bedrock of this nation" was "the belief in things not seen; the belief that there are better days ahead" (Obama, "2004 Democratic Convention Keynote"), accessed March 5, 2010, at www.americanrhetoric.com/speeches/convention2004/barackobama2004dnc.htm). There are similar references affirming faith and drawing inspiration from it in virtually all his subsequent major speeches.

10. "Obama's Nobel Remarks," www.nytimes.com/2009/12/11/world/europe/11 prexy.text.html? accessed March 5, 2010.

11. Ibid. See also Smith (2012).

12. For valuable reflections on this topic that are less favorable to Lincoln than the account here, see Graber (2006).

13. "Remarks by President Obama in Eulogy for the Honorable Reverend Clementa Pinckney,"https://www.whitehouse.gov/the-press-office/2015/06/26/remarks-president-eulogy-honorable-reverend-clementa-pinckney, accessed August 18, 2015.

14. Ibid.

15. "Obama 2004 Democratic National Convention Keynote Address," www .americanrhetoric.com/speeches/convention2004/barackobama2004dnc.htm, accessed September 30, 2009.

16. Ibid.

17. "Obama Announcement Speech," www.guardian.co.uk/world/2007/feb/10/barackobama, accessed September 30, 2009.

18. "Obama's Inaugural Address," www.cnn.com/2009/POLITICS/01/20/obama.politics/index.html, accessed September 20, 2009.

19. "Obama's 2012 Nomination Acceptance Speech," www.presidency.ucsb.edu/ws/index.php?pid=101968, accessed September 10, 2014.

20. "Obama's Second Inaugural address," www.presidency.ucsb.edu/ws/index .php?pid=102827, accessed September 10, 2014.

21. "Transcript of Obama's speech on race," www.msnbc.com/id/23690567/print/1/displaymode/1098/, accessed September 30, 2009.

22. Ibid.

23. See also "A Call to Courage: Reclaiming Our Civil Liberties Ten Years after 9/11." American Civil Liberties Union, https://www.aclu.org/files/assets/acalltocourage.pdf, accessed September 30, 2014.

24. "Glenn Beck: Obama Is Racist," www.cbsnews.com/stories/2009/07/29/oikutucs/main5195604.html, accessed March 11, 2010. See also Christopher (2009).

25. Ricci v. De Stefano, "Opinion of the Court," 25 (2009).

26. "Remarks by the President on a New Beginning," www.whitehouse.gov/the_press_office/Remarks-by-the-President-at-Cairo-University-6-04-09/, accessed March 11, 2010.
27. Ibid.
28. Obama's campaign website can be found via the Internet Wayback Machine: web.archive.org/web/20120107175343/www.barackobama.com/about/barack-obama?source=primary-nav, accessed October 2, 2014.

WORKS CITED

Barone, Michael. 2009. "Obama Lets Congress—and Lobbyists—Do the Work." http://www.washingtonexaminer.com/obama-lets-congress-and-lobbyists-do-the-work/article/100730, April 23, 2009, accessed September 20, 2014.

Bash, Dana, and Emily Sherman. 2009. "Sotomayor's 'Wise Latina' Comment a Staple of Her Speeches." www.cnn.com/2009/POLITICS/06/05/sotomayor.speeches/#cnnSTCTest, accessed September 30, 2009.

Boerma, Lindsay. 2012. "Obama Reflects on His Biggest Mistake as President." *CBS News*, July 12. www.cbsnews.com/news/obama-reflects-on-his-biggest-mistake-as-president/, accessed September 30, 2014.

Boritt, Gabor S. 1978. *Lincoln and the Economics of the American Dream.* Memphis: Memphis State University Press.

Christopher, Tommy. 2009. "Rush Limbaugh Calls Sonia Sotomayor, President Obama 'Racists.'" www.politicsdaily.com/2009/05/26/rush-limbaugh-calls-sonia-sotomayor-president-obama-racists/, accessed March 11, 2010.

Coates, Ta-Nehisi. 2012. "Fear of a Black President." *The Atlantic*, August 22. www.theatlantic.com/magazine/archive/2012/09/fear-of-a-black-president/309064/?single_page=true, accessed September 14, 2014.

Cole, David. 2012. "Obama and Terror: The Hovering Questions." *New York Review of Books*, July 12. www.nybooks.com/articles/archives/2012/jul/12/obama-and-terror-hovering-questions/, accessed October 1, 2014.

Elazar, Daniel J. 1965. "Comment." In *Economic Change in the Civil War Era*, edited by David T. Gilchrist and W. David Lewis. Greenville, DE: Eleutherian Mills-Hagley Foundation.

Fredrickson, George M. 2008. *Big Enough to Be Inconsistent: Abraham Lincoln Confronts Slavery and Race.* Cambridge, MA: Harvard University Press.

Glastris, Paul. 2012. "The Incomplete Greatness of Barack Obama." *Washington Monthly*, March–April. www.washingtonmonthly.com/magazine/

march_april_2012/features/the_incomplete_greatness_of_ba035754.
php?page=all, accessed September 30, 2014.

Graber, Mark A. 2006. *Dred Scott and the Problem of Constitutional Evil*. New York: Cambridge University Press.

Granick Jennifer Stisa, and Christopher Jon Sprigman. 2013. "The Criminal N.S.A." *New York Times*, June 27. www.nytimes.com/2013/06/28/opinion/the-criminal-nsa.html?pagewanted=all&_r=0, accessed October 2, 2014.

Healy, Gene. 2014. "Is Obama Abusing the Constitution to Combat ISIS?" *The National Interest*, September 12. http://nationalinterest.org/feature/obama-abusing-the-constitution-combat-isis-11269, accessed September 30, 2014.

Hickey, Jennifer G. 2014. "Race Gap: Blacks Fall Further Behind under Obama." *Newsmax*, January 8. www.newsmax.com/Newsfront/obama-blacks-poverty-education/2014/01/08/id/545866/, accessed September 30, 2014.

King, Desmond S., and Rogers M. Smith. 2011. *Still a House Divided: Race and Politics in Obama's America*. Princeton, NJ: Princeton University Press.

Korte, Gregory. 2014a. "Obama Didn't Put Up 'Much of a Fight' to Keep Holder." *USA Today*, September 25. www.usatoday.com/story/news/politics/2014/09/25/eric-holder-attorney-general-resigns/16203079/, accessed September 30, 2014.

———. 2014b. "Obama Issues 'Executive Orders by Another Name.'" *USA Today*, December 17. www.usatoday.com/story/news/politics/2014/12/16/obama-presidential-memoranda-executive-orders/20191805/, accessed August 18, 2015.

Lapsley, Arthur Brooks, ed. 1906. *The Writings of Abraham Lincoln*. New York: Lamb Publishing.

Law, Anna O. 2014. "Lies, Damned Lies, and Obama's Deportation Statistics," April 21. www.washingtonpost.com/blogs/monkey-cage/wp/2014/04/21/lies-damned-lies-and-obamas-deportation-statistics/, accessed September 30, 2014.

Liptak, Adam. 2014. "Court Backs Michigan on Affirmative Action." *New York Times*, April 22. www.nytimes.com/2014/04/23/us/supreme-court-michigan-affirmative-action-ban.html?_r=0, accessed September 30, 2014.

McPherson, James B. 1988. *Battle Cry of Freedom: The Civil War Era*. New York: Oxford University Press.

Mendelberg, Tali, and Bennett L. Butler. 2014. "Obama Cares: Look at the Numbers." *New York Times*, August 22.

National Women's Law Center. 2014. "Status of the Lawsuits Challenging the Affordable Care Act's Birth Control Coverage Benefit." www.nwlc.org/status-lawsuits-challenging-affordable-care-acts-birth-control-coverage-benefit, accessed September 30, 2014.

Obama, Barack. 2006. *The Audacity of Hope: Thoughts on Reclaiming the American Dream* (New York: Crown).

———. 2013. "Inaugural Address." January 21. www.whitehouse.gov/the-press-office/2013/01/21/inaugural-address-president-barack-obama, accessed October 2, 2014.

———. 2016. "State of the Union Address." January 12. http://www.nytimes.com/2016/01/13/us/politics/obama-2016-sotu-transcript.html, accessed January 15, 2016.

Packer, George. 2010. "Obama's Lost Year." *The New Yorker*, March 15.

Remnick, Noah. 2014. "What Obama's My Brother's Keeper Initiative Means for Black America." *Los Angeles Times*, July 30. www.latimes.com/opinion/opinion-la/la-ol-obama-brothers-keeper-black-america-20140730-story.html#page=1, accessed October 2, 2014.

Robinson, Eugene. 2010. "On Health Care, Do It." www.realclearpolitics.com/articles/2010/02/23/on_health_care_do_it_104515.html, accessed March 5, 2010.

Ross, Dorothy. 2009. "Lincoln and the Ethics of Emancipation: Universalism, Nationalism, Exceptionalism." *Journal of American History* (September): 379–99. http://jah.oxfordjournals.org/content/96/2/379.extract, accessed March 4, 2010.

Schulten, Susan. 2009. "Barack Obama, Abraham Lincoln, and John Dewey." *University of Denver Law Review* 86: 807–18.

Skocpol, Theda. 1992. *Protecting Soldiers and Mothers*. Cambridge, MA: Harvard University Press.

Smith, Rogers M. 2012. "The Constitutional Philosophy of Barack Obama: Democratic Pragmatism and Religious Commitment." *Social Science Quarterly* 93: 1251–71.

Stolberg, Sheryl Gay, and Robert Pear. 2010. "Obama Signs Health Care Overhaul Bill, With a Flourish." *New York Times*, March 23. www.nytimes.com/2010/03/24/health/policy/24health.html, accessed June 22, 2010.

Street, Paul. 2010. "White America Lives in Vicious Racial Denial—Obama Is Making It Worse." www.neiu.edu/~sociolgy/soc_club_files/white_privlege/Street—10-3-08—White%20America%20&%20Racial%20Denial.pdf, accessed March 7, 2010.

Weiss, Debra Cassens. 2013. "Scalia: Reauthorized Voting Rights Act Was 'Perpetuation of Racial Entitlement.'" *ABA Journal*, February 28. www .abajournal.com/mobile/article/scalia_reauthorized_voting_rights_act_was_ perpetuation_of_racial_entitlemen, accessed September 30, 2014.

Williams, T. Harry, ed. 1957. *Abraham Lincoln: Selected Speeches, Messages, and Letters*. New York: Holt, Rinehart and Winston.

2

TRAJECTORIES OF
MULTICULTURAL CITIZENSHIP

· · · · · · · · · ·

WILL KYMLICKA

INTRODUCTION

Since the late 1960s, debates within the Western democracies about the legal
and political accommodation of ethnic diversity have often been framed as
debates about "multiculturalism." In the last few years, however, an increasing number of commentators have argued that the era of multiculturalism
is over. Indeed, talk about the "rise and fall of multiculturalism" has become
a kind of mantra, widely invoked by scholars, journalists, and policy makers alike to explain the evolution of contemporary debates about diversity.
Although people disagree about what comes "after multiculturalism," there is
a surprising consensus that we are indeed in a "post-multicultural" era.

As with most "rise and fall" historical narratives, the reality is more complex. Both the rise and the fall of multiculturalism have been uneven processes, varying with the specific issues and countries involved, and I believe
that these variations can tell us a great deal about the strengths and limitations of multiculturalism.

In this chapter, I want to focus in particular on the role that citizenship
plays within these debates. I will argue that one crucial factor in explaining the
variable fate of multiculturalism is its perceived link with issues and ideals of
citizenship. This is hardly a novel insight; many of those who defend the "rise

and fall" narrative argue that the main reason for the fall of multiculturalism is its inattention to issues of citizenship. They argue that we need to replace a "multicultural agenda" with a post-multicultural "citizenship agenda."

I will offer a different diagnosis. I will argue that the multiculturalism agenda has always been a citizenship agenda. Multiculturalism has often been promoted as a means of "citizenization" intended to deepen relations of democratic citizenship. Viewing multiculturalism in this way, as a form of citizenship, offers a new lens for thinking about the rise of multiculturalism and its subsequent fate. My goal in this chapter is to offer this alternative account of the trajectory of multiculturalism and its associated ideals of citizenship.

Before doing so, however, it is important to say a bit more about the "rise and fall" narrative that I am contesting, and the role that citizenship plays within it. In its simplest form, the narrative goes like this:[1]

1. From the 1970s to mid-1990s there was a clear trend across the Western democracies toward the increased recognition and accommodation of diversity through a range of multiculturalism policies (MCPs) and minority rights. These policies were endorsed at the domestic level in various states and by international organizations and involved a rejection of earlier ideas of unitary and homogenous nationhood.

2. Since the mid-1990s, however, we have seen a backlash and retreat from multiculturalism, and a reassertion of ideas of nation building, common values and identity, and unitary citizenship—even a "return of assimilation."

3. This retreat is partly driven by fears among the majority group that the accommodation of diversity has "gone too far" and is threatening their way of life. This fear often expresses itself in the rise of nativist and populist right-wing political movements, such as Front National in France, or the Danish People's Party, defending old ideas of "Denmark for the Danish."

4. But the retreat also reflects a belief among the center-left that multiculturalism has failed to help the intended beneficiaries—namely, minorities themselves—because it has failed to address the underlying sources of their social, economic, and political exclusion, and may indeed have unintentionally contributed to their social isolation. As a result, even the center-left political movements that had initially championed multiculturalism,

such as the social democratic parties in Europe, have backed away from it and shifted to a discourse that emphasizes ideas of "civic integration," "social cohesion," "common values," and "shared citizenship."[2]

5. The social-democratic discourse of national integration differs from the radical right discourse in emphasizing the need to develop a more inclusive sense of shared citizenship and national identity, and to fight racism and discrimination, but nonetheless distances itself from the rhetoric and policies of multiculturalism. The term "post-multiculturalism" has often been invoked to signal this new approach, which seeks to overcome the perceived limits of a naive or misguided multiculturalism while avoiding the oppressive reassertion of homogenizing nationalist ideologies.[3]

This narrative is increasingly influential, found not only in academic writings and media commentators but also in the official documents of national governments and international organizations.[4] It does capture some important features of our current situation. At a deeper level, however, I will argue that it misdiagnoses both the rise and the fall of multiculturalism, and as a result, misidentifies the real choices we face. In the rest of the chapter, I will offer a competing account of the rise of multiculturalism and of its uneven retreat, one that tells a very different story about the relationship between multiculturalism and citizenship.

WHAT IS MULTICULTURALISM?

Any account of the trajectory of multiculturalism must begin with some account of the term "multiculturalism." When people talk about the rise and fall of multiculturalism, what exactly is it that is supposed to have risen and fallen? And here, I think, a fundamental problem already starts to emerge. Much of the literature operates with a very limited, even caricatured, view of multiculturalism as essentially a naive and uncritical celebration of ethnocultural diversity. Viewed this way, multiculturalism has little or no substantive connection to ideals of citizenship and may indeed be at odds with basic citizenship values.

In this section, I will explain why I think this account is mistaken, and will offer a different account of the goals and characteristics of multiculturalism, one that ties it more centrally to ideals of citizenship. This alternative account, I will argue, is not only more accurate of real-world multicultural policies and practices but also better explains why it arose in the first place.

According to many of its critics, particularly in the post-multiculturalism literature, multiculturalism is characterized as a feel-good celebration of ethnocultural diversity, encouraging citizens to acknowledge and embrace the panoply of customs, traditions, music, and cuisine that exists in a multiethnic society. Yasmin Alibhai-Brown calls this the "3S" model of multiculturalism in Britain—saris, samosas, and steel drums (Alibhai-Brown 2000). Multiculturalism takes these familiar cultural markers of ethnic groups—clothing, cuisine and music—and treats them as authentic cultural practices to be preserved by their members, and safely consumed as cultural spectacles by others. So they are taught in multicultural school curricula, performed in multicultural festivals, displayed in multicultural media and museums, and so on.

In my view, as I will explain below, this is a caricature of multiculturalism. But it is an influential caricature, and it underpins the idea that promoting multiculturalism is disconnected from promoting citizenship. From a citizenship perspective, the 3S model of multiculturalism suffers from a number of obvious flaws:

1. It entirely ignores issues of economic and political inequality. Even if all Britons come to enjoy Jamaican steel drum music or Indian samosas, this by itself would do nothing to address the real problems facing Caribbean and south Asian communities in Britain—problems of unemployment, poor educational outcomes, residential segregation, poor English language skills, and political marginalization. These economic and political issues cannot be solved simply by celebrating cultural difference.

2. Even with respect to the (legitimate) goal of promoting greater understanding of cultural difference, the focus on celebrating discrete "authentic" cultural practices that are "unique" to each group is potentially dangerous and misleading from a citizenship perspective. First, not all customs that may be traditionally practiced within a particular group are worthy of being celebrated, or even of being legally tolerated, such as forced marriage. To avoid this risk, there's a tendency to choose safely inoffensive practices as the focus of multicultural celebrations—such as cuisine or music—practices that can be enjoyably consumed by members of the larger society. But this runs the opposite risk of the trivialization or Disneyfication of cultural difference (Bissoondath 1994), ignoring the real challenges that differences in cultural values and religious doctrine can raise.

3. The 3S model of multiculturalism can encourage a conception of groups as hermetically sealed and static, each reproducing its own distinct authentic practices. Multiculturalism may be intended to encourage people to share their distinctive customs, but the very assumption that each group has its own distinctive customs ignores processes of cultural adaption, mixing and mélange, and renders invisible emerging cultural commonalities, and thereby potentially reinforces perceptions of minorities as eternally "Other." The result is the perpetuation of stereotypes, which in turn can lead to processes of ethnic polarization, the decline in intergroup trust, and the erosion of solidarity across ethnic, racial, and religious lines.

4. This model can end up reinforcing power inequalities and cultural restrictions within minority groups. In deciding which traditions are "authentic," and how to interpret and display them, the state generally consults the traditional elites within the group—typically older males—while ignoring the way these traditional practices (and traditional elites) are often challenged by internal reformers, who have different views about how, say, a "good Muslim" should act. It can therefore imprison people in "cultural scripts" that they are not allowed to question or dispute. In the name of recognizing or accommodating minority groups, it in fact weakens the position of "internal minorities" within the minority group, such as women and youth.

According to post-multiculturalists, it is the gradual recognition of these flaws that explains the retreat from multiculturalism, and the move toward a new citizenship agenda. This new post-multiculturalist model of citizenship emphasizes:

1. the priority of political participation and economic opportunities over the symbolic politics of cultural recognition,
2. the priority of human rights and individual freedom over respect for cultural traditions,
3. the priority of building inclusive common national identities over the recognition of ancestral cultural identities,
4. the priority of cultural change and cultural mixing over the reification of static cultural differences.

All four of these are described as requiring a shift from a multiculturalism agenda to a citizenship agenda.

If this description were correct—if multiculturalism was fundamentally about celebrating cultural difference in the form of discrete folk practices—then the post-multiculturalist critique would certainly be justified. In my view, however, this is a caricature of the reality of multiculturalism as it has developed over the past forty years in the Western democracies, and a distraction from the real issues we need to face. The 3S model captures something important about natural human tendencies to simplify ethnic differences, and about the logic of global capitalism to sell cosmopolitan cultural products, but it does not capture the nature of post-1960s government multiculturalism policies (MCPs), which had more complex historical sources and political goals.

One problem with the 3S account is that it entirely decontextualizes and depoliticizes multiculturalism, giving us no sense of the political mobilizations that led to the adoption of multiculturalism. Who were the political agents who struggled for multiculturalism, and what were they hoping to achieve by so doing? What was the problem to which multiculturalism was viewed as a potential solution?

In order to understand the nature and specificity of contemporary multiculturalism, we need to recall its political and historical context. In one sense, "multiculturalism" is as old as humanity—different cultures have always found ways of coexisting, and respect for diversity was a familiar feature of many historic empires, such as the Ottoman or Habsburg Empires. But the sort of multiculturalism that is said to have had a "rise and fall" is a much more specific historic phenomenon, emerging first in the Western democracies in the late 1960s. This timing is important, for it helps us situate multiculturalism in relation to larger social transformations of the postwar era.

More specifically, multiculturalism can be seen as part of a larger "human rights revolution" in relation to ethnic and racial diversity. Prior to World War II, ethnocultural and religious diversity in the West was characterized by a range of illiberal and undemocratic relations—including relations of conqueror and conquered, colonizer and colonized, master and slave, settler and indigenous, racialized and unmarked, normalized and deviant, orthodox and heretic, civilized and primitive, ally and enemy. These relationships of hierarchy were justified by racialist ideologies that explicitly propounded the superiority of some peoples and cultures, and their right to rule over others. These ideologies were widely accepted throughout the Western world and underpinned domestic laws (e.g., racially biased immigration and citizenship policies) and foreign policies (e.g., in relation to overseas colonies).

After World War II, however, the world recoiled against Hitler's fanatical and murderous use of such ideologies, and the UN decisively repudiated them in favor of a new ideology of the equality of races and peoples. And this new assumption of human equality has generated a series of political movements designed to contest the lingering presence or enduring effects of older hierarchies. We can distinguish three "waves" of such movements: (a) the struggle for decolonization, concentrated in the period 1948 to 1965; (b) the struggle against racial segregation and discrimination, initiated and exemplified by the African American civil rights movement from 1955 to 1965; and (c) the struggle for multiculturalism and minority rights, which has emerged from the late 1960s.

Each of these movements draws upon the human rights revolution, and its foundational ideology of the equality of races and peoples, to challenge the legacies of earlier ethnic and racial hierarchies. Indeed, the human rights revolution plays a double role here, not just as the inspiration for struggle, but also as a constraint on the permissible goals and means of that struggle. Insofar as historically excluded or stigmatized groups struggle against earlier hierarchies in the name of equality, they too have to renounce their own traditions of exclusion or oppression in the treatment of, say, women, gays, people of mixed race, religious dissenters, and so on. The framework of human rights, and of liberal-democratic constitutionalism more generally, provides the overarching framework within which these struggles are debated and addressed.

Each of these movements, therefore, can be seen as contributing to a process of *democratic citizenization*—that is, turning the earlier catalog of hierarchical relations into relationships of liberal-democratic citizenship, in terms of the vertical relationship between the members of minorities and the state, and in terms of the horizontal relationships among the members of different groups.[5] In the past, it was often assumed that the only way to engage in this process of citizenization was to impose a single undifferentiated model of citizenship on all individuals. But the ideas and policies of multiculturalism that emerged from the 1960s start from the assumption that this complex history inevitably and appropriately generates group-differentiated ethnopolitical claims. The key to citizenization is not to suppress these differential claims but to filter and frame them through the language of human rights, civil liberties, and democratic accountability. And this is what multiculturalist movements have aimed to do.

The precise character of the resulting multicultural reforms varies from group to group, as befits the distinctive history that each has faced. They all start from the antidiscrimination principle that underpinned the second wave, but go beyond it to challenge other forms of exclusion or stigmatization. In most Western countries, explicit state-sponsored discrimination against ethnic, racial, or religious minorities had largely ceased by the 1960s and 1970s, under the influence of the second wave of human rights struggles. Yet evidence of ethnic and racial hierarchies remained, and continues to be clearly visible in many societies, whether measured in terms of economic inequalities, political underrepresentation, social stigmatization, or cultural invisibility. Various forms of multiculturalism have been developed to help overcome these lingering inequalities.

We can broadly distinguish three patterns of multiculturalism that have emerged in the Western democracies. First, we see new forms of empowerment of indigenous peoples, such as the Maori in New Zealand, aboriginal peoples in Canada and Australia, American Indians, Sami in Scandinavia, or Inuit of Greenland. These new models of multicultural citizenship for indigenous peoples often include some combination of the following nine policies:[6]

1. recognition of land rights/title
2. recognition of self-government rights
3. upholding historic treaties and/or signing new treaties
4. recognition of cultural rights (language, hunting/fishing, sacred sites)
5. recognition of customary law
6. guarantees of representation/consultation in the central government
7. constitutional or legislative affirmation of the distinct status of indigenous peoples
8. support/ratification for international instruments on indigenous rights
9. affirmative action

Second, we see new forms of autonomy and power sharing for substate national groups, such as the Basques and Catalans in Spain, Flemish and Walloons in Belgium, Scots and Welsh in Britain, Quebecois in Canada,

Germans in South Tyrol, Swedish in Finland, and so on. These new forms of multicultural citizenship for national minorities typically include some combination of the following six elements:

1. federal or quasi-federal territorial autonomy
2. official language status, either in the region or nationally
3. guarantees of representation in the central government or on Constitutional Courts
4. public funding of minority language universities/schools/media
5. constitutional or parliamentary affirmation of "multinationalism"
6. according international personality (e.g., allowing the substate region to sit on international bodies, or sign treaties, or have their own Olympic team)

And, finally, we see new forms of multicultural citizenship for immigrant groups, which may include a combination of the following eight policies:

1. constitutional, legislative, or parliamentary affirmation of multiculturalism, at the central and/or regional and municipal levels;
2. the adoption of multiculturalism in school curricula;
3. the inclusion of ethnic representation/sensitivity in the mandate of public media or media licensing;
4. exemptions from dress codes, Sunday-closing legislation, and such (either by statute or by court cases);
5. allowing dual citizenship;
6. the funding of ethnic group organizations to support cultural activities;
7. the funding of bilingual education or mother-tongue instruction;
8. affirmative action for disadvantaged immigrant groups.

While there are important differences among these three modes of multicultural citizenship, each of them has been defended as a means to overcome the legacies of earlier hierarchies, and to help build fairer and more inclusive democratic societies.[7]

In my view, therefore, multiculturalism is first and foremost about developing new models of democratic citizenship, grounded in human rights ideals, to replace earlier uncivil and undemocratic relations of hierarchy and exclusion. This account of multiculturalism-as-citizenization differs dramatically from the "3S" account of multiculturalism as the celebration of static cultural differences. Whereas the 3S account says that multiculturalism is about displaying and consuming differences in cuisine, clothing, and music, to the neglect of issues of political and economic inequality, the citizenization account says that multiculturalism is about constructing new civic and political relations to overcome the deeply entrenched inequalities that have persisted after the abolition of formal discrimination.

It is important to determine which of these accounts provides a more accurate description of the Western experience with multiculturalism. Before we can decide whether to celebrate or lament the fall of multiculturalism, or to replace it with post-multiculturalism, we need first to make sure we know what multiculturalism has in fact been. I have elsewhere tried to give a fuller defense of my account (Kymlicka 2007, chaps. 3–5), so let me here just note three ways in which the 3S account is misleading.

First, the claim that multiculturalism is solely or primarily about symbolic cultural politics depends on a misreading of the actual policies. If we look at the three lists of policies above, it is immediately apparent that they combine economic, political, social, and cultural dimensions. Take the case of land claims for indigenous peoples. While regaining control of their traditional territories certainly has cultural and religious significance for many indigenous peoples, it also has profound economic and political significance. Land is the material basis for economic opportunities and political self-government. Or consider language rights for national minorities. According official language status to a minority's language is partly valued as a form of symbolic "recognition" of a historically stigmatized language. But it is also a form of economic and political empowerment; the more a minority's language is used in public institutions, the more its speakers have access to employment opportunities and decision-making procedures. Indeed, the political and economic dimensions of the multiculturalist struggles of indigenous peoples and national minorities are obvious; they are about restructuring state institutions, including redistributing political control over important public and natural resources.

The view that multiculturalism is about the apolitical celebration of ethnic folk customs, therefore, only has any plausibility in relation to immigrant groups. And indeed representations of cuisine, dress, and music are often the most visible manifestations of "multiculturalism" in the schools and media. It is not surprising, therefore, that when post-multiculturalists discuss multiculturalism, they almost invariably ignore the issue of indigenous peoples and national minorities and focus only on the case of immigrant groups, where the 3S account has more initial plausibility.

But even in this context, if we look back at the list of eight multiculturalism policies adopted in relation to immigrant groups, we will quickly see that they too involve a complex mixture of economic, political, and cultural elements. While immigrants are (rightly) concerned to contest the historic stigmatization of their cultures, immigrant multiculturalism also includes policies that are centrally concerned with access to political power and to economic opportunities—for example, policies of affirmative action, mechanisms of political consultation, funding for ethnic self-organization, or facilitated access to citizenship.

All three familiar patterns of multiculturalism, therefore—for indigenous peoples, national minorities, and immigrant groups—combine cultural recognition, economic redistribution, and political participation. In this respect, the post-multiculturalist critique of multiculturalism as ignoring economic and political inequality is simply off the mark.

Second, the claim that multiculturalism ignores the importance of universal human rights is equally misplaced. On the contrary, as we've seen, multiculturalism is itself a human-rights-based movement, inspired and constrained by principles of universal human rights and liberal-democratic constitutionalism. Its goal is to challenge the sorts of traditional ethnic and racial hierarchies that have been discredited by the postwar human rights revolution. Understood in this way, multiculturalism-as-citizenization offers no support for protecting or accommodating illiberal cultural practices within minority groups that have also been discredited by this human rights revolution. The same human-rights-based reasons we have for endorsing multiculturalism-as-citizenization are equally reasons for rejecting cultural practices that violate human rights. And indeed, this is what we see throughout the Western democracies. Wherever multiculturalism has been adopted, it has been tied conceptually and institutionally to larger human rights norms and has been subject to the overarching principles of the liberal-democratic constitutional order (Calma 2007). No Western democracy has exempted immigrant groups from constitutional norms of human rights in order to maintain practices of, say, forced marriage, criminalization of apostasy, or clitoridectomy. Here again, the post-multiculturalist claim that human rights should take precedence over the recognition of cultural traditions simply reasserts what has been integral to the theory and practice of multiculturalism.

And this in turn points out a third flaw in the post-multiculturalists' account—namely, the claim that multiculturalism ignores or denies the reality of cultural change. On the contrary, multiculturalism-as-citizenization is a deeply (and intentionally) transformative project, for minorities and for majorities. It demands both dominant and historically subordinated groups to engage in new practices, to enter new relationships, and to embrace new concepts and discourses, all of which profoundly transform people's identities and practices.[8]

This is obvious in the case of the historically dominant majority nation in each country, which is required to renounce fantasies of racial superiority, to relinquish claims to exclusive ownership of the state, and to abandon attempts to fashion public institutions solely in its own national (typically white/Christian) image. In fact, much of multiculturalism's "long march through the institutions" consists in identifying and attacking those deeply rooted traditions, customs, and symbols that have historically excluded or stigmatized minorities. Much has been written about the transformations in majority identities and practices this has required, and the backlash it can create.[9]

But multiculturalism is equally transformative of the identities and practices of minority groups. Many of these groups have their own histories of ethnic and racial prejudice, of anti-Semitism, of caste and gender exclusion, of religious triumphalism, and of political authoritarianism, all of which are delegitimized by the norms of liberal-democratic multiculturalism and minority rights. It is not only majority populations who have had illiberal and undemocratic tendencies. For all such people, multiculturalism offers both opportunities and challenges. These policies provide clear access points and legal tools for nondominant groups to challenge their status. But there is a price for this access—namely, accepting the principles of human rights and civil liberties, and the procedures of liberal-democratic constitutionalism, with their guarantees of gender equality, religious freedom, racial nondiscrimination, gay rights, due process, and so on. They can appeal to multiculturalism policies to challenge their illiberal exclusion, but those very policies also impose the duty on them to be inclusive.

Moreover, even where the traditional practices of a minority group are free of illiberal or undemocratic elements, they may involve a level of cultural closure that becomes unattractive and unsustainable under multiculturalism.

These practices may have initially emerged as a response to earlier experiences of discrimination, stigmatization, or exclusion at the hands of the majority, and may lose their attractiveness as that motivating experience fades in people's memories. For example, some minority groups have developed distinctive norms of self-help, endogamy, and internal conflict resolution because they have been excluded from or discriminated within the institutions of the larger society. Those norms may lose their rationale as ethnic and racial hierarchies break down, and as group members feel more comfortable interacting with members of other groups and participating in state institutions. Far from guaranteeing the protection of the traditional ways of life of either the majority or minorities, multiculturalism poses multiple challenges to them. Here again, the post-multiculturalists claim about recognizing the necessity of cultural change simply reasserts a long-standing part of the multicultural agenda.

In short, I believe that the post-multiculturalist critique is largely off target, primarily because it misidentifies the nature and goals of the multiculturalism policies and programs that have emerged over the past forty years during the "rise" of multiculturalism, and in particular ignores the way they have been tied to processes of citizenization.

THE FALL OF MULTICULTURAL CITIZENSHIP?

But this then raises a puzzle. If post-multiculturalist claims about the flaws of multiculturalism are largely misguided, and if the multiculturalist agenda was already a citizenship agenda, then what explains the fall of multiculturalism? If, as I claim, multiculturalism is inspired by human rights norms, and seeks to deepen relations of democratic citizenship, why has there been such a retreat from it?

And here emerges my second main point of disagreement with the standard narrative. Just as I believe it has mischaracterized the initial rise of multiculturalism, so too I believe it mischaracterizes the more recent challenges to multiculturalism. The standard narrative both misidentifies the scale of the so-called retreat from multiculturalism and also its underlying causes.

To begin with, reports of multiculturalism's death are very much exaggerated. Here again, we need to keep in mind the different forms that multiculturalism takes, only some of which have faced serious backlash. For example, there has been no retreat from the commitment to new models of multicultural citizenship for indigenous peoples. On the contrary, the trend toward enhanced land rights, self-government powers, and customary law for indigenous peoples remains fully in place across the Western democracy and has been reaffirmed by the UN's General Assembly through the adoption of the Declaration of the Rights of Indigenous Peoples in 2007. Similarly, there has been no retreat from the commitment to new models of multicultural citizenship for national minorities. On the contrary, the trend toward enhanced language rights and regional autonomy for substate national groups remains fully in place in the Western democracies.[10] Indeed, these two trends are increasingly firmly entrenched in law and public opinion, backed by growing evidence that the adoption of multicultural reforms in these contexts has in fact contributed to building relations of democratic freedom and equality.[11] Few people today, for example, would deny that regional autonomy for Catalonia has contributed to the democratic consolidation of Spain, or that indigenous rights are helping to deepen democratic citizenship in Latin America.

So it is only with respect to immigrant groups that we see any serious retreat from multiculturalism. And even here talk of "retreat" is often misleading. Using the Multiculturalism Policy Index discussed earlier, we ranked the strength of immigrant MCPs (multiculturalism policies) across twenty-one OECD (Organisation for Economic Co-operation and Development) countries at three points in time: 1980, 2000, and 2010, and the clear trend has been toward the expansion of MCPs over the last thirty years, including in the past ten years (see the table below, adapted from Banting and Kymlicka 2013). There are some high-profile exceptions: there has been a significant reduction in the Netherlands, and modest ones (from a low base) in Denmark and Italy. But the last decade has also seen a strengthening of immigrant multiculturalism policies in a number of countries, including Belgium, Finland, Greece, Ireland, Norway, Portugal, Spain, and Sweden. In other countries, the scores have increased marginally or remained stable. Overall, the record of immigrant MCPs is one of modest strengthening. As the table indicates, the average score for the twenty-one countries rose from 1.29 in 1980 to 2.71 in 2000 and 3.48 in 2010. Other independent efforts to measure the strength of MCPs in Europe have arrived at the same conclusion.[12]

This may surprise readers given that talk of multiculturalism is so unfashionable in many political circles. But the retreat may indeed be more a matter of talk than of actual policies. Certain politicians in Britain and Australia, for example, have decided to no longer use "the 'm' word," and to talk instead

Immigrant Multiculturalism Policy Scores, 1980–2010

	Total Score (out of a possible 8)		
	1980	*2000*	*2010*
Canada	5	7.5	7.5
Australia	4	8	8
Austria	0	1	1.5
Belgium	1	3	5.5
Denmark	0	0.5	0
Finland	0	1.5	6
France	1	2	2
Germany	0	2	2.5
Greece	0.5	0.5	2.5
Ireland	1	1.5	3
Italy	0	1.5	1
Japan	0	0	0
Netherlands	2.5	5.5	2
New Zealand	2.5	5	5.5
Norway	0	0	2.5
Portugal	1	2	3.5
Spain	0	1	3.5
Sweden	3	5	7
Switzerland	0	1	1
United Kingdom	2.5	5.5	5.5
United States	3	3	3
European Average	**0.7**	**2.1**	**3.1**
Overall Average	**1.29**	**2.71**	**3.48**

Note: Countries could receive a total score of 8, one for each of the following 8 policies: (1) Constitutional, legislative, or parliamentary affirmation of multiculturalism at the central and/or regional and municipal levels and the existence of a government ministry, secretariat, or advisory board to implement this policy in consultation with ethnic communities; (2) The adoption of multiculturalism in school curriculum; (3) The inclusion of ethnic representation/sensitivity in the mandate of public media or media licensing; (4) Exemptions from dress codes; (5) Allowing of dual citizenship; (6) The funding of ethnic group organizations or activities; (7) The funding of bilingual education or mother-tongue instruction; (8) Affirmative action for disadvantaged immigrant groups.

Source: Keith Banting and Will Kymlicka, Multiculturalism Policy Index, www.queensu.ca/mcp.

about, say, "diversity," "pluralism," "intercultural dialogue," or "community cohesion," but these changes in wording have not necessarily affected actual policies and programs on the ground. In Derek McGhee's words, speaking of Britain, "In many ways this retreat from and open hostility to multiculturalism is, on examination, an exercise in avoiding the term 'multiculturalism' rather than moving away from the principles of multiculturalism altogether" (McGhee 2008, 85). In his recent overview of the situation across Europe, Steven Vertovec similarly concludes that while the word *multiculturalism* "has mostly disappeared from political rhetoric," this "has not emerged with the eradication, nor even much to the detriment, of actual measures, institutions and frameworks of minority cultural recognition.... Policies and programs once deemed 'multicultural' continue everywhere" (Vertovec and Wessendorf 2010, 18, 21). Talk of a "wholesale retreat" (Joppke 2004, 244) is, therefore, misleading.[13]

Nonetheless, even if the retreats are more rhetorical than substantive, the abandonment of a multiculturalist rhetoric is revealing and requires some explanation. It suggests a loss of confidence in the multiculturalist agenda, even if no substantive alternative has emerged to take its place. Indeed, this is what I think we are witnessing today—a growing uncertainty about the merits of immigrant multiculturalism, particularly among its erstwhile defenders on the center-left. In most countries, the conservative right was never sympathetic to multiculturalism, and that has not changed. The "rise and fall" of multiculturalism, therefore, is fundamentally a story about the social-democratic or center-left parties and movements. They are the ones who initially pushed for the rise of multiculturalism but who are now having second thoughts about whether it should continue to be seen as a core component of a broader progressive politics. They have not been persuaded that there is some other, better alternative—and hence multiculturalist policies remain largely untouched on the ground—but there is no longer the confidence needed to push the multiculturalist agenda forward, or even to continue to champion it rhetorically. Multiculturalism survives on the ground more from inertia and the lack of clear alternatives than from confident advocacy.

So the question can be rephrased: why has the center-left lost confidence in the immigrant multiculturalist agenda? This is no doubt a complicated question, whose answer is likely to vary from country to country. But in my view, a crucial factor is concern about the potential unintended effects of multiculturalism. Even if, as I've argued, multiculturalism was intended to be a project of citizenization, many people worry that in practice it has set in motion a series of political or sociological processes that have subverted its original intentions. Indeed, the post-multiculturalist literature is full of speculation about such unintended effects. Multiculturalism is said to have exacerbated intergroup stereotyping; reduced levels of intergroup trust and solidarity; weakened the welfare state; encouraged religious radicalization among immigrant youth and nativist anti-immigrant radicalization among the white working class; encouraged the formation of socially isolated ethnic ghettoes; harmed women and other vulnerable members of minority groups; and more generally impeded the effective political, economic, and social integration of immigrants.

Most critics quickly acknowledge that none of these effects were intended or desired by the policy makers who adopted the policies. These are, rather, said to be the unintended perverse effects of a well-intentioned but naive multiculturalism. This emphasis on unintended effects is one of the most striking features of the post-multiculturalist literature, which is full of phrases such as "doing harm by doing good" or "generous betrayal" (to quote two recent book titles on multiculturalism) (Macey 2009; Wikin 2002). As Ruud Koopmans puts it, while its advocates may have had "legitimate normative reasons" for multiculturalism, "we cannot simply assume that what is normatively justifiable will also be practically efficient" (Koopmans 2006, 5), and indeed he argues that multiculturalism has been counterproductive in its effects, subverting its original normative goals. Whereas scholars generally agree that multiculturalism in relation to indigenous peoples and substate national minorities has been successful, the scholarly literature is much more divided in relation to multiculturalism for immigrants. While some scholars argue that multiculturalism has indeed promoted citizenization for immigrants, others have argued that it has unintentionally impeded that process.[14]

Confronted by this barrage of claims of unintended effects, it is not surprising that many erstwhile defenders of multiculturalism have lost their sense of confidence. Yet what is equally remarkable is how little evidence we have for any of these claims. Critics sometimes say that multiculturalism is a "proven failure," but in fact we have nothing like "proof" for any of these alleged perverse effects. Indeed, we have remarkably little evidence one way or another about multiculturalism's effects. Multiculturalism may be eroding intergroup trust, for example, as critics fear, or it may be enhancing trust, as defenders intended—we simply don't know. One can give anecdotes to support either view, or give plausible-sounding sociological speculations to support either view, but we have few studies that actually test the question directly. Surprisingly few researchers have engaged in the sort of longitudinal or cross-national studies that would be needed to isolate the differential effects arising from the adoption of multiculturalism policies, comparing multicultural situations with their non-multicultural or pre-multicultural alternatives.[15] In short, as several recent commentators have observed, we simply do not have the evidentiary base needed for evaluating multicultural-ism (e.g., Marc 2009; Reitz 2009).[16]

Under these circumstances, the ambivalent nature of the current "retreat" from immigrant multiculturalism becomes more understandable. According to its post-multiculturalist critics, (1) multiculturalism is characterized by a commitment to a naive 3S-style celebration of diversity, (2) multiculturalism is a proven failure, and (3) this failure has led to a widespread retreat from multiculturalism. But in fact none of these claims is accurate. Multicultural-ism is about citizenization, not about celebrating diversity for its own sake, and while it is not a proven failure neither is it a proven success, leading to uncertainty about its actual effects. The result has been a progressive loss of confidence in the multiculturalist agenda, but little or no substantive retreat from its actual practices.

If this analysis is correct, it is too early to predict the long-term trajec-tory of multicultural citizenship. In the short term, in the absence of reliable evidence, we are likely to continue to witness debates characterized by fear mongering and reckless speculation rather than by reasonable deliberation. Nativists and populists have proven adept at manipulating these fears, in ways that I believe are threatening the progress that has been made in build-ing more inclusive models of citizenship. The striking rise of far-right anti-immigrant parties is the most visible manifestation of these disturbing trends.

In the longer term, however, there is some prospect that we will be able to more accurately judge what is working and what is not in the multicultur-alist agenda. Indeed, I think that the evidence is already starting to emerge, if only in a fragmentary way. And while the evidence is incomplete, I believe it offers cautious grounds for optimism.

As we've seen above, post-multiculturalists argue that immigrant multi-culturalism has (unintentionally) impeded citizenization by generating a series of perverse effects, including:

exacerbating intergroup stereotyping;
diminishing trust and bonding social capital between ethnic groups;
eroding the sense of solidarity needed for the welfare state;
displacing attention from issues of political participation and economic
    inequality.

In the past few years, a number of studies have emerged that allow us to begin testing these speculations. I have reviewed this evidence elsewhere (Kymlicka 2010), but let me briefly and schematically summarize some of the key findings. Contrary to the post-multiculturalist claims, the evidence from cross-national studies suggests that:

stereotyping is lower not higher in countries with strong immigrant multi-
    culturalism policies (Weldon 2006; Guimond et al. 2013);
while increasing immigration is associated with declining trust and social
    capital across many countries (Putnam 2007), this effect is weaker, and in
    some cases reversed entirely, in countries with immigrant multicultural-
    ism policies (Kessler and Bloemraad 2010), in part because multicultural-
    ism serves to "normalize" diversity (Kazemipur 2009; Harrell 2009);
countries with strong immigrant multiculturalism polices have done at least
    as well, if not better, in sustaining their welfare states than countries with
    weaker or nonexistent multiculturalism (Banting and Kymlicka 2006);
while immigrants in all Western countries are disadvantaged in the labor
    market and underrepresented in their access to political power, the size
    of this "ethnic penalty" is lowest in countries with strong immigrant
    multiculturalism policies, both in relation to the labor market (Heath
    2007) and political participation and representation (Bloemraad 2006;
    Adams 2007).

In short, recent cross-national studies show a consistent pattern in which the adoption of multiculturalism is associated with benign or even positive outcomes on those issues that post-multiculturalists claim it generates bad outcomes—stereotyping, trust and solidarity, economic opportunities, and political participation.

I hasten to emphasize again that these recent studies are in many cases a first preliminary effort to test the underlying claims, often using data that are incomplete or imperfect. Future research may well require some adjust-ment in these findings. And of course these studies do not yet tell us what are the underlying causal mechanisms at work—that is, they do not tell us the causal mechanisms by which the adoption of multiculturalism policies shapes underlying social processes of stereotyping, trust building, civic participa-tion, labor market integration, and so on. It would not be surprising if future research revealed that multiculturalism polices affected stereotyping or social trust through multiple causal chains, some beneficial and some pernicious, the specificity of which is lost in these aggregate cross-national studies.

But notwithstanding the serious limitations of the research, it seems clear to me that post-multiculturalist claims about the unintended perverse effects of multiculturalism are unsupported by the bulk of the research done to date, and appear to be vastly overstated.[17] At the very least, we have no grounds for saying that the experiment in multicultural citizenship has been proven a failure and may yet discover that, in at least some respects, it is proving to be beneficial.

CONCLUSION: THE FUTURE OF MULTICULTURAL CITIZENSHIP

If this analysis is correct, it has important implications for the future of multicultural citizenship. On the one hand, despite all the talk about the retreat from multiculturalism, it suggests that multiculturalism in general has a bright future. There are powerful forces at work in modern Western societies pushing in the direction of the public recognition and accommodation of ethnocultural diversity. Public values and constitutional norms of tolerance, equality, and individual freedom, underpinned by the human rights revolution, all push in the direction of multiculturalism, particularly when viewed against the backdrop of a history of ethnic and racial hierarchies.

These forces have proven decisive in at least some contexts of ethnic diversity, particularly regarding the rights of substate national groups and indigenous peoples. Older ideas of undifferentiated citizenship and neutral public spheres have collapsed in the face of these trends, and no one today seriously proposes that these forms of minority rights and differentiated citizenship for historic minorities could be abandoned or reversed.[18] That minority rights, liberal democracy, and human rights can comfortably coexist is now a fixed point in domestic constitutions and in international law. There is no credible alternative to multiculturalism in these contexts.

The situation with respect to immigrant groups is more complex. The same factors that push for multiculturalism in relation to historic minorities have also generated a willingness to contemplate multiculturalism for immigrant groups, and indeed such policies seem to have worked well under some conditions. However, confidence in immigrant multiculturalism has been eroded by serious anxieties about a range of potential perverse effects. I have suggested that these anxieties are overstated, and unsupported by the research to date, but they remain matters of live concern, and the result has been a kind of paralysis of the multiculturalist agenda. Immigrant multiculturalism is no longer championed rhetorically, but neither is it abandoned in practice.

It is too early to tell how this paralysis will be overcome, and whether multicultural citizenship will be able to effectively address these existential worries. But we cannot even begin to make progress on this question if we start from the current master narrative of the rise and fall of multiculturalism. That narrative, I have argued, misidentifies the nature of multiculturalism, its link to citizenship, and its results in practice.

NOTES

1. For influential academic statements of this "rise and fall" narrative, claiming that it applies across the Western democracies, see Brubaker (2001); Joppke (2004); cf. Baubock (2002). There are also many accounts of the "decline," "retreat," or "crisis" of multiculturalism in particular countries, such as Netherlands (Entzinger 2003; Koopmans 2006; Prin and Slijper 2002; Britain (Hansen 2007; Back et al. 2002; Vertovec 2005); Australia (Ang and Stratton 2001; Poynting and Mason 2008); and Canada (Wong, Garcea, and Kirova 2005).

2. For an overview of the attitudes of European social democratic parties to these issues, see Cuperus, Duffek, and Kandel (2003).

3. For references to "post-multiculturalism" by progressive intellectuals and academics, who distinguish it from the radical right's "anti-multiculturalism," see Alibhai-Brown (2000, 2004, re the United Kingdom); Jupp (2007, regarding Australia); King (2004); Hollinger (2006 re the United States).

4. See, for example, Council of Europe 2008.

5. I adapt the term citizenization from Tully (2000). As Tully emphasizes, citizenization is not just about extending formal citizenship to minorities, in part because this can be done in a unilateral and paternalistic way. (This is how Canadian citizenship was extended to Aboriginal peoples in 1960.) Citizenization, rather, involves a willingness to negotiate as equals the terms of belonging with the goal of reaching consent. In the case of indigenous peoples, this may include the willingness to consider challenges to the state's legitimacy and jurisdiction, which were initially imposed by force on colonized groups. In that sense, citizenization is not only more than formal citizenship; it can also include challenges to state citizenship, as when some Aboriginal leaders insist they never consented to being Canadian citizens. As long as the goal is to replace coercion and paternalism with democratic consent and to replace

hierarchy with nondomination, then we have citizenization. For related discussions in the African context of how challenges to state citizenship regimes in the name of substate nationalisms or suprastate federalism can themselves be expressions of the process of democratic citizenization, see Smith (2013, on Ethiopia); Cooper (2014, on French West Africa). As the Smith book indicates, a form of citizenization can take place even when the larger political system is authoritarian not liberal-democratic. In this chapter, however, I focus on multiculturalism and citizenization within the consolidated Western democracies.

6. This and the following lists of multicultural policies are taken from the Multiculturalism Policy Index first published in Banting and Kymlicka (2006) and updated in Banting and Kymlicka (2013). The Index is available at www.queensu.ca/mcp.

7. There was briefly in some European countries a form of "multiculturalism" that was not aimed at the inclusion of permanent immigrants, but rather at ensuring that temporary migrants would return to their country of origin. For example, mother-tongue education in Germany was not initially introduced "as a minority right but in order to enable guest worker children to reintegrate in their countries of origin" (Schönwälder 2010, 160). This sort of "returnist" multiculturalism—premised on the idea that migrants are foreigners who should return to their real home—has nothing to do with multiculturalism policies premised on the idea that immigrants belong here, and which aim to make immigrants feel more at home here. My focus is on the latter type of multiculturalism, which I argue is centrally concerned with constructing new relations of citizenship.

8. "Nothing has changed more over thirty years of identity politics than the identities of men and women, immigrants and old-timers, indigenous and non-indigenous persons, Muslims and Christians, Arabs and Westerners, Europeans and non-Europeans, cultural minorities and majorities, heterosexuals and homosexuals" (Tully 2000, 231).

9. For a discussion of "white backlash" against multiculturalism, see Hewitt (2005).

10. The backlash against the Roma in parts of Europe is a complicated exception, in part because they do not fit neatly into the category of either "national minority" or "immigrant." On the general trends regarding the rights of indigenous groups and national minorities, and the ambiguous state of the Roma in relation to them, see Kymlicka 2007.

11. I survey the evidence in Kymlicka (2007, chap. 5).

12. Koopmans's index of Indicators of Citizenship Rights for Immigrants (ICRI) includes both an individual equality/nondiscrimination dimension and a multiculturalism dimension, with twenty-three different indicators for the multiculturalism dimension. Developed independently, the consistency between his ICRI results and our MCP Index results helps confirm the trend we both observe. See Koopmans, Michalowski, and Waibel (2012).

13. The real policy change has not been the abandonment of multiculturalist policies, but rather (1) the tightening of admission policies (e.g., more restrictive rules regarding refugee determination or family reunification); and (2) the adoption of new "civic integration" policies, which require immigrants to take various courses and to pass various tests in order to maintain their residency or to become citizens. For a mapping of these civic integration policies, see Goodman (2010, 2014). Although these reforms are often described as replacing a multiculturalism agenda with a citizenship or integration agenda, the evidence shows that civic integration policies have not replaced preexisting multiculturalism policies, but rather have been layered on top of them. Moreover, if we examine the content of these civic integration policies more carefully, we find that they tend to mirror the preexisting level of commitment to multiculturalism. That is to say, countries with strong multiculturalist policies promote a multiculturalist conception of citizenship in their civic integration policies (see the comparison of Canadian and Danish citizenship tests in Adamo 2008). For more on the different ways that multiculturalism policies and civic integration policies can either fit together or conflict, see Banting and Kymlicka (2013).

14. For example, while studies have shown that immigrant multiculturalism policies in Canada have had strongly beneficial effects in relation to citizenization (Bloemraad 2006), other studies suggest that immigrant multiculturalism in the Netherlands has had deleterious effects (Koopmans et al. 2005; Sniderman and Hagendoorn 2007). I discuss these Dutch studies in Kymlicka (2008).

15. For one important exception, see Kesler and Bloemraad (2010), which measures the impact of immigrant MCPs across nineteen countries, and argues that they have had modest positive effects.

16. According to Reitz, while academic discussions of multiculturalism have been extensive, "there is no real evaluation. The information base for such an evaluation is simply not there" (Reitz 2009, 13).

17. In many cases, the post-multiculturalists blame multiculturalism for social ills that in fact predate the adoption of multiculturalism, and which

are found in equal (if not greater) measure in countries without multiculturalism. Few if any post-multiculturalists make the effort needed to identify
the differential effects of having multiculturalism policies.

18. Even a fierce critic of multiculturalism like Brian Barry (2001) makes no
attempt to apply his ideas to the case of substate national groups and indigenous peoples.

WORKS CITED

Adamo, Silvia. 2008. "Northern Exposure: The New Danish Model of Citizenship Test." *International Journal on Multicultural Societies* 10 (1): 10–28.

Adams, Michael. 2007. *Unlikely Utopia: The Surprising Triumph of Canadian
Pluralism.* Toronto: Viking.

Alibhai-Brown, Y. 2000. *After Multiculturalism.* London: Foreign Policy
Centre.

———. 2003. "Post-Multiculturalism and Citizenship Values." Presented to
Immigrant Council of Ireland Conference on Immigration, Ireland's Future,
December 11.

———. 2004. "Beyond Multiculturalism." *Canadian Diversity / Diversité Cana-
dienne* 3 (2): 51–4.

Ang, I., and J. Stratton. 2001. "Multiculturalism in Crisis: The New Politics of
Race and National Identity in Australia." In *On Not Speaking Chinese: Living between Asia and the West,* edited by I. Ang, 95–111. London: Routledge.

Back, L., M. Keith, A. Khan, K. Shukra, and J. Solomos. 2002. "New Labour's
White Heart: Politics, Multiculturalism, and the Return of Assimilation."
Political Quarterly 73: 445–54.

Banting, Keith, and Will Kymlicka. 2013. "Is There Really a Retreat from
Multiculturalism Policies? New Evidence from the Multiculturalism Policy
Index." *Comparative European Politics* 11 (5): 577–98.

Banting, Keith, and Will Kymlicka, eds. 2006. *Multiculturalism and the Welfare
State: Recognition and Redistribution in Contemporary Democracies.* Oxford:
Oxford University Press.

Barry, Brian. 2001. *Culture and Equality: An Egalitarian Critique of Multiculturalism.* Cambridge: Polity Press.

Baubock, Rainer. 2002. "Farewell to Multiculturalism? Sharing Values and
Identities in Societies of Immigration." *Journal of International Migration
and Immigration* 3: 1–16.

Berry, John, Jean Phinney, David Sam, and Paul Vedder. 2006. *Immigrant Youth
in Cultural Transition.* Mahwah, NJ: Lawrence Erlbaum Associates.

Bissoondath, Neil. 1994. *Selling Illusions: The Cult of Multiculturalism in Canada.* Toronto: Penguin.

Bloemraad, Irene. 2006. *Becoming a Citizen: Incorporating Immigrants and Refugees in the United States and Canada.* Berkeley: University of California Press.

Brubaker, Rogers. 2001. "The Return of Assimilation?" *Ethnic and Racial Studies* 24 (4): 531–48.

Calma, Tom. 2007. *Multiculturalism: A Position Paper by the Acting Race Discrimination Commissioner.* Human Rights and Equal Opportunity Commission, Government of Australia. www.hreoc.gov.au/racial_discrimination/multi culturalism/index.html.

Cooper, Frederick. 2014. *Citizenship between Empire and Nation: Remaking France and French Africa.* Princeton, NJ: Princeton University Press.

Council of Europe, Committee of Ministers. 2008. "White Paper on Intercultural Dialogue." Council of Ministers 30, May 2.

Cuperus, R., K. Duffek, and J. Kandel, eds. 2003. *The Challenge of Diversity: European Social Democracy Facing Migration, Integration, and Multiculturalism.* Innsbruck: Studien Verlag.

Entzinger, Han. 2003. "The Rise and Fall of Multiculturalism in the Netherlands." In *Toward Assimilation and Citizenship: Immigrants in Liberal Nation-States,* edited by C. Joppke and E. Morawska, 59–86. London: Palgrave.

Goodman, Sara. 2010. "Integration Requirements for Integration's Sake? Identifying, Categorizing, and Comparing Civic Integration Policies." *Journal of Ethnic and Migration Studies* 36 (5): 753–72.

———. 2014. *Immigration and Membership Politics in Western Europe.* Cambridge: Cambridge University Press.

Guimond, S., et al. 2013. "Diversity Policy, Social Dominance, and Intergroup Relations: Predicting Prejudice in Changing Social and Political Contexts." *Journal of Personality and Social Psychology* 104 (6): 941–58.

Hansen, R. 2007. "Diversity, Integration, and the Turn from Multiculturalism in the United Kingdom." In *Belonging? Diversity, Recognition, and Shared Citizenship in Canada,* edited by K. Banting, T. Courchene, and L. Seidle, 35–86. Montreal: Institute for Research on Public Policy.

Harell, Allison. 2009. "Minority-Majority Relations in Canada: The Rights Regime and the Adoption of Multicultural Values." Paper presented at the Canadian Political Science Association Annual Meeting, Ottawa, ON. http://cpsa-acsp.ca/papers-2009/Harell.pdf.

Heath, Anthony. 2007. "Crossnational Patterns and Processes of Ethnic Disadvantage." In *Unequal Chances: Ethnic Minorities in Western Labour Markets,* edited by Anthony Heath and Sin Yi Cheung. Proceedings of the British Academy 137. Oxford: Oxford University Press.

Hewitt, Roger. 2005. *White Backlash and the Politics of Multiculturalism*. Cambridge: Cambridge University Press.

Hollinger, David. 2006. *Postethnic America: Beyond Multiculturalism*. Rev. ed. New York: Basic Books.

Joppke, Christian. 2004. "The Retreat of Multiculturalism in the Liberal State: Theory and Policy." *British Journal of Sociology* 55 (2): 237–57.

Jupp, James. 2007. *From White Australia to Woomera: The Story of Australian Immigration*. 2nd ed. Cambridge: Cambridge University Press.

Kazemipur, Abdolmohammad. 2009. *Social Capital and Diversity: Some Lessons from Canada*. Bern: Peter Lang.

Kesler, Christel, and Irene Bloemraad. 2010. "Does Immigration Erode Social Capital? The Conditional Effects of Immigration-Generated Diversity on Trust, Membership, and Participation across 19 Countries, 1981–2000." *Canadian Journal of Political Science* 43 (2): 319–47.

King, Desmond. 2004. *The Liberty of Strangers: Making the American Nation*. Oxford: Oxford University Press.

Koopmans, Ruud. 2006. "Trade-Offs between Equality and Difference: The Crisis of Dutch Multiculturalism in Cross-National Perspective." Brief, Danish Institute for International Affairs, December.

Koopmans, Ruud, Ines Michalowski, and Stine Waibel. 2012. "Citizenship Rights for Immigrants: National Political Processes and Cross-National Convergence in Western Europe, 1980–2008." *American Journal of Sociology* 117 (4): 1202–45.

Koopmans, R., P. Statham, M. Guigni, and F. Passy. 2005. *Contested Citizenship: Immigration and Cultural Diversity in Europe*. Minneapolis: University of Minnesota Press.

Kymlicka, Will. 2004. "Marketing Canadian Pluralism in the International Arena." *International Journal* 59 (4): 829–52.

———. 2007. *Multicultural Odysseys: Navigating the New International Politics of Diversity*. Oxford: Oxford University Press.

———. 2008. "Review of Paul Sniderman and Louk Hagendoorn's *When Ways of Life Collide: Multiculturalism and Its Discontents*," *Perspectives on Politics* 6 (4): 804–7.

———. 2010. "Testing the Liberal Multiculturalist Hypothesis: Normative Theories and Social Science Evidence." *Canadian Journal of Political Science* 43 (2): 257–71.

Macey, Marie. 2009. *Multiculturalism, Religion, and Women: Doing Harm by Doing Good?* New York: Palgrave Macmillan.

Marc, Alexandre. 2009. *Delivering Services in Multicultural Societies.* Washington, DC: World Bank.

McGhee, Derek. 2008. *The End of Multiculturalism? Terrorism, Integration, and Human Rights.* New York: Open University Press.

OECD. 2006. Where Immigrant Students Succeed—A Comparative Review of Performance and Engagement in PISA 2003. OECD, Program for International Student Assessment.

Poynting, Scott, and Victoria Mason. 2008. "The New Integrationism, the State, and Islamophobia: Retreat from Multiculturalism in Australia." *International Journal of Law, Crime, and Justice* 36: 230–46.

Prins, Baukje, and Boris Slijper. 2002. "Multicultural Society under Attack." *Journal of International Migration and Immigration* 3 (3): 313–28.

Putnam, Robert. 2007. "E Pluribus Unum: Diversity and Community in the Twenty-First Century." *Scandinavian Political Studies* 30 (2): 137–74.

Reitz, Jeffrey. 2009. "Assessing Multiculturalism as a Behavioural Theory." In *Multiculturalism and Social Cohesion: Potentials and Challenges of Diversity,* edited by Raymond Breton, Karen Dion, and Kenneth Dion, 1–48. London: Springer.

Schönwälder, Karen. 2010. "Germany: Integration Policy and Pluralism in a Self-Conscious Country of Immigration." In *The Multiculturalism Backlash: European Discourses, Policies, and Practices,* edited by Steven Vertovec and Susanne Wessendorf. London: Routledge.

Smith, Lahra. 2013. *Making Citizens in Africa: Ethnicity, Gender, and National Identity in Ethiopia.* Cambridge: Cambridge University Press.

Sniderman, Paul., and L. Hagendoorn. 2007. *When Ways of Life Collide.* Princeton, NJ: Princeton University Press.

Tully, James. 2000. "The Challenge of Reimagining Citizenship and Belonging in Multicultural and Multinational Societies." In *The Demands of Citizenship,* edited by Catriona McKinnon and Iain Hampsher-Monk. London: Continuum.

Vertovec, S. 2005. "Pre-, High-, Anti-, and Post-Multiculturalism." ESRC Centre on Migration, Policy and Society, University of Oxford.

Vertovec, Steven, and Susan Wessendorf, eds. 2010. *The Multiculturalism Backlash: European Discourses, Policies, and Practices.* London: Routledge.

Weldon, Steven. 2006. "The Institutional Context of Tolerance for Ethnic Minorities." A 3

3

POLITICAL ACTIVISM
"OF" OR "FOR" MIGRANTS?

· · · · · · · · · ·

Classification Struggles in the Korean Migrant Worker
Advocacy Movement

NORA HUI-JUNG KIM

The question of nation-state membership is a complicated one and involves at least two dimensions of membership. The first dimension is access to formal citizenship, which corresponds to the state part of the nation-state. The second dimension is the issue of national inclusion, which corresponds to the nation part of the nation-state. Every nation-state has officially established requirements for acquiring formal membership, but what qualifies an individual (or a group of people) as a legitimate member of a nation often depends on symbolic representation. This chapter explores the contested nature of symbolic citizenship using South Korea's (hereafter Korea) migrant worker advocacy movement as a case study. The migrant worker advocacy movement in Korea is a particularly interesting case to study the

Portions of the section "War by Proxy and the Ongoing Classification Struggle" appear in "Multiculturalism and the Politics of Belonging: The Puzzle of Multiculturalism in South Korea," *Citizenship Studies* 16, no. 1 (2012): 103–17.

significance and challenges of representation and how representation is tied to the legal membership.

MIGRANT WORKERS IN KOREA AND THEIR CHALLENGES

Korea has started to accept migrant workers since in the mid-1990s. Currently, a typical migrant worker in Korea is a blue-collar worker in the manufacturing industry from Southeast Asia. Migrant workers are recruited mainly via the Employment Permit System (EPS), which was introduced in 2004. According to the Korean Immigration Service (KIS), a total of 61,064 new EPS visas were issued in 2013, about 92 percent of which were issued to male workers (KIS 2013, 276). Currently there are fifteen countries that have a Memorandum of Understanding (MOU) with the Korean government to send migrant workers to Korea. Some of the top sending countries include Vietnam, Cambodia, Nepal, Indonesia, and the Philippines. Foreign workers of Korean descent (mainly from China) constitute another important pool of migrant workers. However, they are not recruited via EPS but via family and relative visitation visas. On paper, migrant workers of Korean descent are not "migrant workers" but "coethnics (*dongpo*)" visiting their motherland. As of December 2013, it is estimated there are about 499,000 (classified as "unskilled") migrant workers, and about 13 percent of them are overstayed or illegal migrants (KIS 2013, 284). The ratio between foreign workers and those of Korean descent is about half and half (Ministry of Justice 2013).

Visa types are not the only or the most significant differences between migrant workers and migrant workers of Korean descent. There is little interaction or cooperation between the two groups of migrant workers. Even advocacy organizations are split between those who work mainly with migrant workers and those who focus on migrant workers of Korean descent. They face different sets of struggles and the struggles of representation unfold in diverging ways. For the consistency of the discussion, this chapter will focus on nonethnic Korean migrant workers only, not migrant workers of Korean descent.

Migrant workers via EPS can stay and work in Korea up to four years and ten months. The maximum length of stay is set that way to prevent migrant workers from claiming formal Korean citizenship. One of the requirements of naturalization in Korea is five years of uninterrupted residency. Further, Korea's long-held myth of ethnic homogeneity has justified denying "nonpure" Koreans full membership. For example, ethnic Chinese residents (*hawgyo*), despite their more than century-long residency in Korea, are treated as "temporary visitors" and have to renew their visitor visa every three years (Lee 2003). While ethnic Chinese residents have been eligible for permanent residency since 2002, application for naturalization still remains very restrictive and challenging for them (Kim 2012, 2013). Mixed-race Koreans (*honhyul*) carry Korean passports but have been marginalized in Korea (Gage 2007; Lee 2008). Their exemption from mandatory military service clearly illustrates their second-class citizenship status (Moon 2005). To claim membership in the Korean nation-state in any meaningful way, migrant workers have to challenge the existing ethnic nationalism that has been used to justify marginalization of ethnic Chinese residents or mixed-race Koreans.

In addition to the lack of access to legal citizenship and the prevalence of ethnic nationalism, migrant workers in Korea face a third challenge in asserting their citizenship. Racial and ethnic exclusivity is often intertwined with national and global hierarchy; Koreans feel superior to people of the third world or developing countries (Nadia Kim 2008). As such, migrant workers in Korea face triple layers of exclusion; they are often darker-skinned than typical Koreans (*ethnic/racial Other*), mainly work in blue-collar occupations that Koreans shun away from (*class Other*), and whose home countries' economic performance is not quite on a par with that of Korea (*national Other*).

Against this background, migrant worker advocacy movements face a daunting task of representing migrant workers as worthy members of Korea. Further, there is disagreement on how to achieve the task, between Korean activists representing migrants and migrants representing themselves and between different groups of migrants. This chapter delves into the struggle over representation of migrant workers and focus on two related aspects. First, I document the struggles (1) between migrant activists and Korean activists on behalf of migrants and (2) among migrant workers. These tensions focus on *how* to represent and *who* has the right to represent migrant workers in Korea. Second, I illustrate the intensification of this ongoing struggle in the context of increasing references to multiculturalism, or what I call the multicultural explosion in Korea. Korea has experienced transformations in both discourse and policy regarding multiculturalism in recent years (Kim 2012). The new discourse on multiculturalism implies that Korea is becoming, or should become, a multicultural society. The multicultural explosion is rather unexpected given the strong myth of ethnic homogeneity. In some sense, the multicultural explosion is a welcome change to the migrant worker advocacy movement as it opens up the possibility of accepting nonethnic Koreans as full members of Korea. However, even in multiculturalism discourse, Korean activists on behalf of migrant workers represent migrants as those who deserve only sympathy, but not respect. Migrant activists, on the other hand, believe that the multiculturalism discourse only perpetuates the negative classification of migrants as less-than-full members of the Korean nation-state. In response, migrant activists attempt to repudiate the legitimacy of Korean activists as actors who represent the interests of migrants; at the same time, migrant activists offer an alternative representation of themselves as a class-conscious laborer. However, not every migrant welcomes this alternative representation, which leads to tension among migrant workers.

My analysis builds on the notion of classification struggle (Bourdieu 1991; Goldberg 2004; Swartz 1997)—the contentious process of making, remaking, and unmaking social groups. The Korean case highlights the importance of representation in the politics of immigration and citizenship. Whether or not immigrants are entitled to and are willing to acquire citizenship—as a legal membership or a symbolic membership—depends in large part on the process and outcome of classification struggles. The data for this chapter come from various sources. The primary sources include government policy documents, statements, and interviews with key informants. These data were collected during the initial seven-month fieldwork from February to August 2006 and one- to two-month fieldworks in the following years. During the main fieldwork, I volunteered at two migrant worker advocacy organizations—the Joint Committee for Migrants in Korea (JCMK) and the Ansan Migrants' Center (AMC)—two days a week at each organization. Both organizations are headed and staffed by Korean activists. I had opportunities to observe the day-to-day activities of Korean activists and their interaction with government officials and migrants. In addition, I attended public hearings—two organized by the Ministry of Justice and one organized by the Ministry of Labor—and posthearing informal gatherings. Attending these meetings provided insight into the policy negotiation process between Korean activists and government officials. To document migrant workers, I conducted formal and informal interviews with them, including two leaders of the Migrant Worker Trade Union. Formal interviews with migrant workers were conducted as a part of a larger study commissioned by the Gyeonggi Research Institute (GRI). The study collected over three hundred questionnaires and conducted thirty in-depth interviews with migrant workers in the Gyeonggi Province (for the full report see GRI 2006). I participated in the study as one of the investigators.

CLASSIFICATION STRUGGLE, REPRESENTATION, AND CITIZENSHIP

Recent years have witnessed increasing political mobilization by migrants in most labor-receiving countries (Koopmans et al. 2005; Ireland 1994; Wihtol de Wenden 1994). The notion of classification struggle can facilitate a more nuanced understanding of migrant political activism. Classification struggle refers to struggles over social categories of belonging (Bourdieu 1984; Swartz 1997), that is, the process of categorizing individuals into a social group with certain characteristics and properties that are distinctive from other social groups. Social groups—whether based on age, sex, ethnicity, class, or skill—are constructed through classification; properties associated with a particular group are also distributed via classification (Bourdieu 1984). This social categorization is politically significant to the extent that such categorization produces a hierarchy among groups, often as a result of the government's differential treatment. In this sense, the classification struggle approach shows how the construction of certain group identities is both a means and a goal of migrant political activism (Brubaker 1992).

The legitimacy of claims associated with classification struggles depends mainly on two factors: The first concerns the social properties of the group in question; the other has to do with the symbolic authority of those who claim to represent that particular group. Feminist activists, for example, have to prove that women as a group deserve rights equal to those of men (Alexander 2003). In addition, those who make claims on behalf of women have to establish their authentic affiliation with women, lest their claims be discredited (Heller 1998).

For migrant political activism, classification involves two types of struggle. The first type is a between-group classification struggle, that is, the struggle between institutional actors and migrants. The second type is a within-group classification struggle, that is, the struggle among migrants over which categories should represent them. While classification struggles appear in various social movements or alongside any type of claims-making on behalf of a collectivity (Alexander 2003; Bourdieu 1984; Goldberg 2004), these struggles assume a particular importance for migrant political activism.

As Bourdieu notes, "struggles over ethnic or regional identity—in other words, over properties (stigmata or emblems) linked with the *origin* through the *place* of origin and its associated durable marks, such as accent—are a particular case of the different struggles over classifications, struggles over the monopoly of power . . . *to make and unmake groups*" (Bourdieu 1984, 221; emphasis in original).

The social characteristics of migrants constructed in and through classification struggles will influence whether and how migrants are to be incorporated into the hosting nation-state. As such, how to represent and who has the authority to represent migrants are essential dimensions of the politics of migration. As Brubaker (1992) aptly reminds readers, migrant political activism is not only about "who gets what" but more importantly is about "who is what." Defining "who is what" concerns the identity aspect of citizenship. Citizenship as identity "refers to the behavioral aspects of individuals acting and conceiving of themselves as members of [a] collectivity, classically the nation, or the normative concepts of such behavior imputed by the state" (Joppke 2007, 38). In order to claim legitimate membership, both formal and symbolic, migrants not only have to meet formal requirements, they also have to cross the symbolic boundary between "them" and "us." To facilitate this process, migrants may adopt certain cultural traits that signify full membership while at the same time trying to distance themselves from groups who possess certain cultural traits considered profane by the nationals (Wimmer 2009).

Migrants' efforts alone are often not sufficient, however; they need to be accepted by the majority population as well (Wimmer 2009, 256). This is because members of the national majority possess symbolic capital that migrants lack—the characteristic of full membership in the nation-state. This symbolic capital awards those in the national majority with authority and legitimacy in envisioning the boundaries of the nation-state and thus endows them with the symbolic power to define whether or not and how migrants are included in the nation-state. As a response, migrants try to impose their own vision of migrants as a group. By doing so, migrants challenge not only the properties assigned to them by national majorities but also the very authority of national majorities to represent migrants as a group.

However, the alternative representation migrant activists promote is also a classification, categorizing individuals into certain social groups. In the course of rejecting the categories assigned by the national majority (between-group classification struggles), migrant activists may impose certain symbolic representations of migrants while suppressing other representations (within-group classification struggles). In what follows, I analyze the ongoing classification struggles between Korean institutional actors and migrant activists and illustrate how this struggle has recently intensified in the context of an unexpected multicultural explosion in Korea.

WAR BY PROXY AND THE ONGOING CLASSIFICATION STRUGGLE

In 2006 when the multicultural explosion started, political activism on the issue of migration in Korea was largely the action of three organizations: the Joint Committee for Migrants in Korea (JCMK), the Network for Migrants' Rights (NMR), and the Migrants' Trade Union (MTU). Both JCMK and NMR can be categorized as national majority groups or institutional actors; both are nongovernmental organizations (NGOs) run by Korean activists, and both maintain a close relationship with the Korean government.[1] The support of the Korean government provides these two NGOs with the resources and power needed to influence migrants' political activism. In contrast, the MTU, a trade union of and by migrant workers, represents immigrant minority actors.

Korean activists working on behalf of migrants are not direct beneficiaries of their activism, but rather constitute allies. For migrant activists, having allies in a movement involves both costs and benefits. The most significant benefit is the allies' influence on the Korean government and migration policies. The Korean government still refuses to acknowledge the MTU as a legitimate partner. For example, the Ministry of Labor has refused to issue a labor union permit for the MTU on the grounds that the majority of its members are illegal workers.[2] In addition, migrants are not invited to any government-initiated policy discussions. Only Korean migration experts (scholars and Korean activists on behalf of migrants) and interested bodies (business owners) are invited to participate as discussants. Thus, without Korean activists working as allies to represent migrants, migrants would be able to achieve very few desired policy changes.

However, the presence of allies creates tension as well. Defining the relationship between Korean activists and migrants has become a source of increasing tension (Lee 2005; Seol 2000). Korean activists have assumed the roles of agent, representative, and spokesperson for migrants. In the context of the Korean government and employers refusing to engage in a dialogue with migrant workers, Korean activists are fighting the war against exploitation and discrimination as proxies for migrants. This creates a *war by proxy* scenario (Dahlstedt and Hertzberg 2007; Radtke 1999), in which migrant workers' interests and voices are channeled through Korean activists' interpretation. The war by proxy situation seemed inevitable given the institutional constraints imposed upon migrant workers. Initially, migrant workers were recruited under the Industrial Trainee System (ITS). Under ITS, migrant workers were considered merely trainees, not workers. As trainees, they were denied important labor rights and quite often suffered inhumane treatment (Lim 2006; Seol 2000) Although ITS was replaced by the Employment Permit System (EPS), which acknowledges migrant workers as laborers, migrant workers in Korea remain vulnerable to deportation and exploitation (Nora Kim 2008).

The between-group classification struggle unfolds around defining the relationship between Korean activists and migrants. Korean activists represent migrants as victims of ill-intended policies and the ethnocentric sentiments of Koreans. On the other hand, Korean activists often portray themselves as a caring father and the migrants as his immature children. For example, when a committee of Korean activists described the arrest of one of their prominent leaders, they noted that he "has been taking care of foreign workers like *a father* would have done."[3] The following excerpt describes the view of migrant workers Korean activists adopt: migrant workers, just like children, need more time to mature to become competent political actors.

> It's too early for migrant workers to take leading roles in the politi-
> cal struggle, because the national division among migrant workers
> hinders them from communicating. In addition, they are still yet
> to acquire their consciousness and they lack resources or skills for
> political mobilization. (Excerpt from *Contemporary Migrant Workers*
> by JCMK, 2001)

Public discussion forums are one social site in which migrants are deprived of their agency and asked by Korean activists to assume the negative representation of dependent and helpless. Korean activists sometimes invite migrant workers to accompany them to government-initiated policy forums. The migrants are stationed behind the Korean activists to add graphic effect to the statements the Korean activists articulate.[4] In Korean NGO-initiated public seminars, migrants play more significant roles than they do in government-initiated forums. However, their role is usually limited to opening the public seminars by testifying about the difficulties they face as minorities in Korea. In both cases, migrants are being objectified as suffering figures whose subjectivity and agency go unnoticed.

Certainly there is a strategic dimension to Korean activists' presentation of migrants as those who are in need of help and victimized. By portraying migrants as those who are too weak to pose a serious threat to the status quo, Korean activists can more effectively bring about policy changes by gaining sympathy from the Korean public and political elites.[5] Nonetheless, these strategic considerations do not fully account for Korean activists' representation of migrants in this manner. Korean activists' practice of classifying migrants as weak subjects also stems from the activists' habitual and subconscious schema regarding migrants as ethnic, class, and national Other. Two observations regarding Korean activists support this point. First, migrant empowerment was not a major concern among Korean activists until the late 1990s. The issue of empowering migrants and acknowledging their capacity to bring about changes on their own came to the fore only when an increasing number of migrant activists started to question the legitimacy of Korean activists as their representatives. Second, evidence can be found in the daily interactions between Korean activists and migrants. Counseling centers, or migrant advocacy NGOs, provide a physical space where migrants and Korean activists interact with one another.[6] Their daily interaction at the counseling centers clearly demonstrates the hierarchy between Korean activists and migrants. By a way of example, migrants address Korean activists as "sir/madam" (*sŏnsaeng-nim*) or "pastor"; these terms are typical appellations used to address superiors or seniors in the Korean context. On the other hand, Korean activists address migrants as "*~ssi*," which is a Korean suffix used to address equal or lower-status individuals, or they address migrants by first name only. These practices symbolize the hierarchical relationship between Korean activists and migrants.

Intentionally and unintentionally, Korean activists exercise symbolic power to define who Koreans and migrants are and to categorize them hierarchically based on ethnicity, class status, and nationality. Korean activists on behalf of migrants represent themselves as "messiahs" against the "oppressor" Koreans such as employers and the Korean government. Korean activists represent migrants as "oppressed" and "victims"; migrant workers are "to be saved" by Korean activists who often have college degrees and come from middle-class backgrounds. In doing so, the hierarchy between Koreans and migrants is confirmed and reproduced. Korean activists' use of class, ethnic, and national privilege has unintended consequences in that it reproduces the very privileges that they initially set out to overcome through their activism. To a certain extent, the Korean activists' treatment of migrants reflects the paternalistic nature prevalent in Korean politics and social movements. However, combined with a sense of superiority based on nationality, ethnicity, and class, the tone of paternalism is much deeper in migrant advocacy movements than in other social movements in Korea.

Against this background, one of the important goals for migrant activism in Korea is to challenge the negative categories imposed by the Korean government and Korean activists on behalf of migrants. A MTU leader noted that:

Before we started this political struggle [public demonstration against the introduction of Employment Permit System], most Koreans, and even our Korean allies, considered us not so much as laborers as those in desperate need of help. But, our struggle has changed their views on us. We are not just poor, incompetent "foreign" workers any more. They now see us as competent, rights-consciousness laborers. That's why the Korean labor union movement now supports our struggles and accepts us as equal comrades. (Speech by an MTU leader, February 24, 2004)

As this quote indicates, against the previous categories of "poor, incompetent foreign workers," migrant activists impose a new classification scheme for migrants as competent class-conscious laborers. Adopting different forms of address during daily interaction with Korean activists is another way migrant activists reclassify themselves vis-à-vis Korean activists. Migrant activists tend to address Korean activists as "comrade" rather than "sir/madam." This indicates migrant workers' efforts to reject the assigned category of inferior and to assert a new category of equal.

In addition, the introduction of EPS triggered this new form of classification struggle—the struggle over delegation. Indeed, the delegation of symbolic power, that is, the power to speak for and represent the group, is at the very center of the classification struggle approach (Bourdieu 1991; Swartz 1997). The contentious process regarding foreign worker policy reform revealed how the interests of Korean activists and migrant activists diverged. In 2001, the Korean government announced the introduction of the EPS to replace the previous Industrial Trainee System. This was a response to the political activism of Korean and migrant activists. Migrant activists decided not to accept the government-proposed EPS, arguing that the policy still privileges Korean employers over migrant workers. They continued protesting and demanding a work visa system. In contrast, Korean activists argued that the EPS policy was good enough and stopped protesting (Nora Kim 2008; Lee 2005). Having realized that Korean activists would not represent migrants' best interests, migrant activists felt the need of representing their own voices independent of that of Korean activists. As one way of doing so, migrant activists pressured the JCMK to change its name from the Joint Committee *of* Migrant Workers in Korea to the Joint Committee *for* Migrant Workers in Korea (Lee 2005). By emphasizing that the JCMK is not *of* migrants, migrant activists discredit the symbolic power of the JCKM to represent migrant workers. The classification struggle to reject the category of "the negative Other" and give voices to migrants also led to the emergence of a migrant-run independent media movement around that time (Lee 2007). Migrant Workers Television and MigrantsInKorea.net are two leading organizations in the arena of political struggle over *who* gets to represent migrant workers.

In short, the war by proxy scenario led to between-group struggles between the Korean activists and the migrant activists. This symbolic struggle has unfolded largely in two dimensions: the struggle regarding the social characterization of migrants (those in need versus competent self-reliant actors) and the struggle over who may authentically represent the migrants' interests (Korean activists versus migrants). These two issues are related; migrant activists contend that they are forced to assume negative characterizations because the role of representing migrants is delegated solely to Korean activists.

MULTICULTURALISM AS THE SITE OF BETWEEN-GROUP CLASSIFICATION STRUGGLE

This ongoing between-group classification struggle is only intensified in the context of the recent multicultural explosion. The number of news articles containing the term "multicultural (*damunhwa*)" increased rapidly in the past few years. While there were only 235 total entries for the entire decade from 1990 to 1999, there were 196 in 2005, 469 in 2006, and 1,252 in 2007.[7] This multicultural trend has reached policy as well; the Multicultural Family Support Act was introduced in 2007. Some specific measures in this policy include: the provision of multicultural education for government officials and employers, the introduction of antidiscrimination laws, and the offering of free Korean culture/language classes. Indeed, the interest in multiculturalism, as indicated by the volume of media coverage and government policies targeting immigrants and ethnic minorities, is so sudden and explosive that it resembles "the multicultural explosion" (Glazer 1997) in the 1990s in the United States.[8]

Korean activists on behalf of migrants also adopted multiculturalism as their primary mode of political claims-making in relation to the Korean government. For example, two migrant advocacy NGOs in Korea changed their organization names to indicate their commitment to multiculturalism; the two agencies are now known as the Multicultural Open Society and the Multicultural Village without Borders. Based on data from the news article search, eighteen organizations have been newly created or restructured so that they have a division devoted to immigrant incorporation.

Initially, Korean activists' interests in multiculturalism and the transition toward a multicultural Korean nation were negligible. As indicated in the quote below, Korean activists assumed that migrants would not want to stay in Korea, and thus multiculturalism was not an attractive option for making claims on behalf of migrants.

> In the course of attending a seminar in Japan entitled, "How to Achieve the Incorporation of Migrant Workers into a Multicultural Society?" one stark difference between migrant workers in Japan and Korea came to mind. In Japan, migrant workers consider Japan a place to settle down. Compared to them, migrant workers in Korea consider Korea a temporary station before their final destination. Migrant workers in Japan are not interested in such programs assisting immigrant workers to return to their home countries. (A statement by a Korean activist; in JCMK Annual Report of 1999)

Japanese activists working on behalf of migrants in Japan employed the phrase "multicultural-commensalism" as a guiding vision for political activism from the start of the movement. Korean activists, on the contrary, focused on protecting the labor rights of migrants during their stay in Korea and providing assisted-return programs, on the assumption that migrants are temporary visitors, not settlers, in Korea. Advocating a transition to a multicultural nation was not a strategically attractive choice. However, it is worth noting that the strategic decision to focus on return programs rather than incorporation programs was based on the Korean activists' interpretation of migrant workers' intentions or interests rather than the latter's true intentions. Korean activists' recently developed interest in multiculturalism developed in part because they finally realized that temporary migrants would not or could not return to their home countries.

However, the more significant catalyst for Korean activists' interest in multiculturalism comes from the Korean government's involvement in the task of incorporating (certain) migrants. The Korean government recently implemented migrant incorporation policies under the rubric of multiculturalism. In this government-sponsored multiculturalism, the main target group is female marriage-based migrants from Southeast Asian countries. The government's involvement in incorporating foreign brides facilitated changes in the activities of migrant advocacy NGOs. The Korean government relies on NGOs to identify foreign brides' policy needs and implement multicultural incorporation programs. The Korean government is more likely to fund activities that assist foreign bride incorporation than those that encourage the incorporation of migrant workers. Thus, by redirecting their focus from migrant workers to foreign brides and by framing their activities as promoting multiculturalism in Korea, migrant advocacy NGOs are able to acquire more funding from the Korean government and increase their organizational capacity. The recent multicultural explosion was born out of this collaboration between the Korean government and migrant advocacy NGOs.

The multicultural explosion has had a negative impact on migrant workers and their ongoing classification struggle vis-à-vis Korean activists. There are only a few multicultural policies regarding migrant workers in Korea. Even in migrant-worker-targeted multicultural programs, the participation and representation of migrants are limited. Migrant workers in Korea "are simply mobilized to various government-organized events. They do not either express opinions on multiculturalism or initiate multicultural events of their own" (Lee 2007, 103). Thus most migrant workers are skeptical of the multicultural explosion, as indicated in the following quote from an interview:

> From the beginning to the end, Koreans controlled every aspect of *Migrants' Arirang*. Just displaying exotic cultures won't bring Koreans and migrant workers closer. Cooperation and communication [in the process] are essential to achieve the aim. If the festival continues to run like it does now, no migrant workers would be interested in participating in the festival anymore. (Author interview with an MTU member, July 2006)

The migrant activist expressed that his disapproval of the multicultural event is due to the lack of representation of migrants. In this sense, the ways in which institutional actors promote multiculturalism perpetuate the marginalization and silencing of migrant workers and their negative categorization.

In addition to the perpetuated objectification and marginalization of migrant workers by Korean activists, a new hierarchical classification scheme emerged as the result of the multicultural explosion. In this new classification scheme, foreign brides, who are characterized as having the potential to assimilate into Korean culture, are prioritized over migrant workers. Korean NGOs now pay less attention to issues germane to migrant workers (for example, introducing a work visa and legalizing undocumented workers) than they have in the past. A survey concerning the current and future activities of fifty-five migrant advocacy NGOs confirms this decline. While 87 percent of NGOs reported that they are providing problem solving by addressing labor or immigration issues, the percentage of NGOs that plan to continue this activity in the future is only 60 percent (Seol and Yi 2006, 34). The percentage of NGOs working on multicultural family or marriage-based migrant assistance in the present and the future remain almost the same, at 54 percent and 56 percent respectively. Moreover, the survey shows increasing interest among migrant advocacy NGOs in the education of children of foreign brides, with 20 percent of the organizations currently addressing this issue and 36 percent planning to work on this issue in the future (Seol and Yi 2006, 34). As such, migrant worker issues are further marginalized in the mist of multicultural explosion.

Given these characteristics of Korean multiculturalism and its impact on the ongoing classification struggle between migrants and Korean activists, it is not surprising that migrant activists are indifferent toward and even critical of the recent shift to multiculturalism. The MTU is particularly censorious of the multicultural explosion because a typical member of the MTU, an undocumented male migrant worker, is positioned at the bottom of the migrant hierarchy and most negatively represented.

Representation is inherently tied to formal, as well as symbolic, citizenship. Being uninvited to even the multicultural Korean nation-state, few migrant workers indicated interest in acquiring Korean citizenship (GRI 2006).[9] Some immigrant workers promote postnational belonging rather than seeking membership in the Korean nation. One of the interviewees expressed such an opinion when he said, "I don't think I have a particular nationality or citizenship anymore. That's true for a lot of migrant workers. We do not belong to either Korea or the country of origin" (author interview with a migrant activist, July 2006).

WITHIN-GROUP CLASSIFICATION STRUGGLE: UNORGANIZED MIGRANT WORKERS VERSUS MTU MEMBERS

The MTU does not represent the entire migrant population in Korea. Rather, they represent a small, but organized and politically mobilized, subgroup of migrants. Most migrants are involved in various national associations. These groups focus on organizing associational life outside the workplace, and most are not politically active. There are in-group classification struggles between the MTU and these national associations; the MTU strives to impose a particular characterization on migrants in Korea: militant, class-conscious laborers.

However, not all migrants support this categorization. Some migrants are not aware of the MTU. Some migrants also do not feel the need to join the MTU given the ample support they receive from their coethnic groups. A Bengali migrant worker interviewee confirms this case. When asked about the MTU, he replied, "I know MTU and I've been there a couple of times. I think they are fine but I just don't consider myself being a member. I have a lot of friends here in Masuk [the name of community where he lives] and I don't need support from others" (author interview, May 2006). Some migrants are simply afraid of the consequences of supporting the MTU or becoming politically active. Because the Korean government closely watches politically active migrant workers, a migrant worker who joins MTU runs

the risk of being ostracized from his or her own national association. An anec-
dote supports this point. A Bengali union activist was told by a Bengali restaurant owner not to come to his restaurant any more. The restaurant owner
argued that a union activist visit to the restaurant would bring the entire
Bengali community in that region under the suspicion of the Korean government (quoted in Lee 2005, 49).

Still others refuse to join or support the MTU because they are critical
of what the MTU represents, as the following interviewee suggests.

> I know that there is MTU. I had met them at public demonstrations.
> When I was the [Filipino] community leader, I've asked a lot to par-
> ticipate in the demonstrations. It [demonstration] works in some
> cases but not in other cases. They need to be creative [with their tac-
> tics]. (Author interview with a Filipino migrant worker, June 2006)

Many migrants who are critical of the MTU do not consider "class-
conscious laborer" an ideal category to represent migrants in Korea. By
imposing its own characterization of migrants (as class-conscious laborers),
the MTU is imposing its own interpretation of the division of the world.
In this sense, migrant activists are engaging in classification struggles not
only vis-à-vis Korean activists (between-group struggle) but also vis-à-vis
in-group members (within-group struggle).

CONCLUSION

I have analyzed the dynamics between migrant activists and their Korean
counterparts and among migrant worker themselves. The ongoing classification struggle between migrant activists and their Korean counterparts has
only intensified in the context of the recent multicultural explosion initiated
by the Korean government and Korean activists. The multiculturalism discourse in Korea creates a new hierarchy among migrants; foreign brides are
prioritized over migrant workers. In response, migrant activists delegitimize
Korean activists as their representatives and present an alternative representation of themselves as class-conscious laborers. However, this new representation is a contested one, grouping migrant workers with diverse ethnicities,
nationalities, and interests into a single category.

The classification struggles between migrant minorities and national
majorities have significant implications for determining migrants' legitimate

membership (Wimmer 2009). The Korean case sheds new light on the relationship between citizenship and representation in two important ways: it provides an arena for examining *how* immigrants are represented and *who* represents immigrants. Indeed, these are two central aspects of a classification struggle. Whether or not immigrants are entitled to and are willing to acquire citizenship—as a legal status and as an identity—depends on *how* immigrants are represented. Unlike foreign brides, who have access to Korean citizenship as wives and mothers of Koreans, migrant workers are categorized as guests and are not offered formal citizenship. Migrant workers, who are represented as incompetent and immature children, do not actively seek Korean citizenship themselves either. In this sense, a lack of fair representation discourages some immigrants from acquiring formal membership.

The Korean case also reveals the importance of *who* has the right to represent whom. Korean activists argue that migrant workers have yet to acquire the skills and abilities needed to represent themselves. The Korean government's denial of the MTU as a legitimate political actor is another obstacle that migrant activists must overcome in order to achieve the right to represent themselves. In addition, the MTU must reach out to more migrant workers if the organization claims to represent migrant workers' collective interests.

Without a doubt, the issues of *how* to represent and *who* represents are related, as the case of migrant workers in Korea illustrates. Even in the context of the multicultural explosion, the unfavorable representation of migrants persists. Migrants, who are rarely allowed to represent themselves, are given the choice to either accept the multiculturalism promoted by Korean activists or to refuse to be a part of multiculturalism at all. Migrant workers choose the latter.

NOTES

1. There are about 155 migrant advocacy organizations in Korea. About a third of the organizations belong to either the JCMK (forty-one member organizations as of 2006) or the NMR (fourteen member organizations as of 2006); the rest operate as independent organizations without any affiliation. Those that are not affiliated with either the JCMK or the NMR are mainly missionary organizations. These organizations provide religious services and a place for migrant workers to meet each other. I limit the current discussion to three main actors (JCMK, NMR, and MTU) because other migrant advocacy organizations are not political (they are mainly missionary

organizations) and do not make any significant statements about multiculturalism (Seol 2000).

2. On June 25, 2015, the Supreme Court of South Korea finally acknowledged the rights of migrant workers to unionize and thus legalized the MTU (case no. 2007DU4995).

3. Excerpt from a statement by the Temporary Committee on Pastor Kim Detention, 1996. The leader, Pastor Hae Sung Kim, is the head of Sŏngnam Migrant Workers' Counseling Center. He was arrested when he protested against the police who tried to investigate the counseling center concerning an allegation that the center provides shelter for undocumented migrant workers (Moon 2000).

4. Attending these public forums is one of the least favorite things to do among migrants because their limited Korean language proficiency makes it difficult for them to understand the debates among Koreans. Even if they do not like it, migrant workers feel obliged to attend when they are asked to do so. Both migrants and Korean activists consider this a matter of reciprocity. Since Korean activists are doing something for migrants, the latter are obligated to do something for Korean activists in return.

5. According to Schneider and Ingram (1993), there are four possible policy target groups: those who are advantaged, contenders, dependents, and deviants. Advantaged groups are powerful and positively constructed, while the contenders are powerful but negatively constructed. Dependent groups are politically weak but generally positive. Finally, deviants are in the worst situation because they are constructed as weak and negative (Schneider and Ingram 1993, 335–36). Facing four possible options when constructing an image of migrant workers, Korean activists choose the category of dependents rather than deviants or contenders.

6. Migrants come to counseling centers to seek legal help and advice, to meet other migrants, or to attend various services (Korean language class, religious services, etc.). These counseling centers function as hubs for immigrants to socialize and make friends. I conducted participation observation study at two counseling centers as a volunteer between February and August 2006.

7. I used the news article search engine service provided by the Korean Press Foundation (www.kinds.or.kr). This search engine's database includes 181 newspapers, both national and local. I counted all the news articles regardless of where and how many times the word *multicultural* appears in an article.

8. Glazer noticed both the recent and explosive usage of the word *multiculturalism* in the United States, observing that "almost every book in the

Harvard University libraries listed as containing the word 'multiculturalism' in its title in the 1970s and 1980s is Canadian or Australian. . . . But here in America, the word multiculturalism is a newcomer" (Glazer 1997, 8). Similarly, in South Korea, the word *multiculturalism* appears only recently. The increase in the usage of multiculturalism in the Korean media is indeed explosive.

9. Ethnic Chinese residents show similar attitudes toward Korean legal citizenship (see Kim 2012).

WORKS CITED

Alexander, Jeffrey C. 2003. *The Meanings of Social Life*. New York: Oxford University Press.

Bourdieu, Pierre. 1984. *Practical Reason*. Stanford, CA: Stanford University Press.

———. 1991. *Language and Symbolic Power*. Cambridge, MA: Harvard University Press.

Brubaker, Rogers. 1992. *Citizenship and Nationhood in France and Germany*. Cambridge, MA: Harvard University Press.

Dahlstedt, Magnus, and Fredrik Hertzberg. 2007. "Democracy the Swedish Way? The Exclusion of 'Immigrants' in Swedish Politics." *Scandinavian Political Studies* 30: 175–203.

Gage, Sue-Je Lee. 2007. "The Amerasian Problem: Blood, Duty, and Race." *International Relations* 21 (1): 86–102.

Glazer, Nathan. 1997. *We Are All Multiculturalists Now*. Cambridge, MA: Harvard University Press.

Goldberg, Chad A. 2004. "Haunted by the Specter of Communism: Collective Identity and Resource Mobilization in the Demise of the Workers Alliance of America." *Theory and Society* 32: 725–73.

Gyeonggi Research Institute (GRI). 2006. Policy Research Report 2006–11: Residency Status of Foreign Workers and Their Needs for Administrative Services.

Heller, Agnes. 1998. "Self-Representation and the Representation of the Other." In *Blurred Boundaries: Migration, Ethnicity, Citizenship*, edited by Rainer Bauböck and John Rundell, 341–54. Aldershot: Ashgate Publishing.

Ireland, Patrick. 1994. *The Policy Challenge of Ethnic Diversity*. Cambridge, MA: Harvard University Press.

Joppke, Christian. 2007. "Transformation of Citizenship: Status, Rights, Identity." *Citizenship Studies* 11 (1): 37–48.

Kim, Nadia Y. 2008. *Imperial Citizens: Koreans and Race from Seoul to LA*. Stanford, CA: Stanford University Press.

Kim, Nora Hui-Jung. 2008. "Korean Immigration Policy Changes and the Political Liberals' Dilemma." *International Migration Review* 42: 576–96.

———. 2012. "Multiculturalism and the Politics of Belonging: The Puzzle of Multiculturalism in South Korea." *Citizenship Studies* 16 (1): 103–17.

———. 2013. "Flexible but yet Inflexible: Development of Dual Citizenship in South Korea." *Journal of Korean Studies* 18 (1): 7–28.

Korean Immigration Service (KIS), Ministry of Justice. 2013. KIS Statistics 2013. ISSN 2005-0356.

Koopmans, Ruud, Paul Statham, Marco Giugni, and Florence Passy. 2005. *Contested Citizenship*. Minneapolis: University of Minnesota Press.

Lee, Chul-Woo. 2003. "'US' and 'THEM' in Korean Law." In *East Asian Law: Universal Norms and Local Cultures*, edited by A. Rosett, L. Cheng, and M. Y. K. Woo, 106–36. London: RoutledgeCurzon.

Lee, Mary. 2008. "Mixed Race Peoples in the Korean National Imaginary and Family." *Korean Studies* 32: 56–85.

Lee, S. O. 2005. "Han'gukesŏŭi iju nodongja undonggwaŭi hyŏngsŏnggaw sŏngkyŏk pyŏnhwa" (The Formation and Effect of Korean-Style Migrant Worker Movement). Master's thesis, Sungkonghoe University.

———. 2007. "Han'gukesŏŭi iju nodongundonggwa *Tamunhwajuŭi*" (Korean-Style Migrant Worker Movement and Multiculturalism). In *Han'gukesŏŭi Tamunhwajuŭi: Hyŏnsilgwa chaengchŏm* (Multiculturalism in South Korea: A Critical Review), edited by Kyungsuk, 82–107. Seoul: Hanul Books.

Lim, Timothy C. 2006. "NGOs, Transnational Migrants, and the Promotion of Rights in South Korea." In *Local Citizenship in Recent Countries of Immigration*, edited by Takeyuki Tsuda, 253–69. New York: Lexington Books.

Ministry of Justice, Republic of Korea. 2013. A Study on Foreign Workers: Work and Social Life of Foreigner Workers via Employment Permit System and Relative Visitation Visa. Publication No. 11-1270000-000802-01 (in Korean).

Moon, Katharine H. S. 2000. "Strangers in the Midst of Globalization: Migrant Workers and Korean Nationalism." In *Korea's Globalization*, edited by Samuel S. Kim, 147–69. New York: Cambridge University Press.

Moon, Seungsook. 2005. *Militarized Modernity and Gendered Citizenship in South Korea*. Durham, NC: Duke University Press.

Oh, Kyungsuk. 2007. "Ŏttŏn *Tamunhwajuŭi* in'ga?" (What Kinds of Multiculturalism?). In *Han'gukesŏŭi Tamunhwajuŭi: Hyŏnsilgwa chaengchŏm*

(Multiculturalism in South Korea: A Critical Review), edited by Kyungsuk Oh, 22–56. Seoul: Hanul Books.

Radtke, Frank-Olaf. 1999. "The Formation of Ethnic Minorities and the Transformation of Social into Ethnic Conflicts in a So-Called Multi-Cultural Society: The Case of Germany." In *Ethnic Mobilization in a Multi-Cultural Europe*, edited by John Rex and Beatrice Drury, 30–47. Brookfield: Avebury.

Schneider, Anne, and Helen Ingram. 1993. "Social Construction of Target Populations: Implications for Politics and Policy." *American Political Science Review* 87 (2): 334–47.

Seol, Dong-Hoon. 2000. "Past and Present of Foreign Workers in Korea, 1987–2000." *Asia Solidarity Quarterly* 2: 6–31.

Seol, Dong Hoon, and Ran Joo Yi. 2006. *Partnership between the Government, Municipalities, and NGOs for Migrant Workers in Korea*. Seoul: Korean Labor Welfare Corporation.

Swartz, David. 1997. *Culture and Power*. Chicago: University of Chicago Press.

Wihtol de Wenden, Catherine. 1994. "Immigrants as Political Actors in France." *Western European Politics* 17: 91–101.

Wimmer, Andreas. 2009. "Herder's Heritage and the Boundary-Making Approach: Studying Ethnicity in Immigrant Societies." *Sociological Theory* 27 (3): 244–70.

Comparative Multilevel Analysis of Western Europe." *American Journal of Political Science* 50 (2): 331–49.

Wikan, Unni. 2002. *Generous Betrayal: Politics of Culture in the New Europe*. Chicago: University of Chicago Press.

Wong, L., J. Garcea, and A. Kirova. 2005. "An Analysis of the 'Anti- and Post-Multiculturalism' Discourses: The Fragmentation Position." Prairie Centre for Excellence in Research on Immigration and Integration, Edmonton, Alberta.

4

TRIPLE MINORITIES REPRESENTING
MAJORITY INTERESTS

· · · · · · · · · ·

TERRI SUSAN FINE

INTRODUCTION

On January 10, 1985, Democrat Madeline Kunin became the seventy-seventh, and the first female, governor of Vermont. She served three consecutive two-year terms and left office in 1991. Before being elected governor, Kunin served as lieutenant governor for two terms and as a representative in the Vermont legislature. Kunin is the only person in the United States to be elected governor three times. More than fifteen years later, in the fall of 2002, Republican Linda Lingle was elected to become the sixth governor of Hawaii, and its first female governor. She served in that office until 2010. Before being elected governor, Lingle served two terms as mayor of Maui County and two terms as a member of the Maui County Council. Lingle was the first, and youngest, woman elected mayor of Maui County. In addition to being elected the first female governors of their respective states, Kunin and Lingle are also the only two Jewish women to ever be elected governor. As elected officials who are members of both gender and religious minorities, Kunin and Lingle demonstrated unlikely success in an electoral and political system organized around majorities.

This study focuses on the demographic and political characteristics of Jewish female state legislators, who, as members of multiple minority groups, have been able to overcome structural, political, and electoral barriers to become state-level policy makers. In addition to being gender and religious minorities, most Jewish women are Democrats, a political minority, while they also compose a numerical minority (whether due to their religion, gender, or party affiliation) in state legislatures. Consequently, Jewish female state legislators are members of three, often four, minority groups. In focusing on Jewish female legislators' demographic and political characteristics, we can develop a stronger understanding of how minorities function in majoritarian political environments.

One unique characteristic of the US electoral system is that it is organized around single member legislative districts (SMD). Each voter casts a single vote for any given office and candidates must secure a plurality of votes in order to get elected. Non-US Western democracies use proportional representation systems to elect members of the legislature.

Two related consequences emerge from single member district systems that differ from proportional representation systems. The first consequence is that SMD systems result in candidates from no more than two parties getting elected, as it is quite difficult to emerge first from a multicandidate field. And voters and financial supporters often support the victor and that victor's party in subsequent elections for various reasons including name recognition, familiarity with the incumbent/incumbent party, and evidence of electoral success. Such incumbency advantages make it difficult for minor parties to secure the needed funding and support to mount competitive campaigns. The second consequence is that the two dominant parties, as they continue winning elections, will then organize the policy-making process in the legislature to the exclusion of minority-party perspectives. In proportional representation systems, voters select from among several political parties and vote for a party, and not individual candidates. Representation in the legislature is then based on the percentage of the vote that each party receives in the election provided that a minimum percentage of the vote, often as little as 5 percent, is earned by that party in the election. As a result, multiple parties of varying strengths can secure representation in the legislature, which encourages coalition building and multiple perspectives being reflected in public policy. By contrast, SMD systems, such as that found in the United States, discourage minority voices from pursuing electoral opportunities because their chances of success are limited by the structural consequences of SMD systems. Even though pluralities are required to win elections in

SMD systems, most of the time it is two candidates from the two major parties vying for a single seat where one emerges the winner with a majority (50 percent or more) of the vote. As a result, majorities are advantaged in electoral processes and in the organization of legislatures in SMD systems such as in the United States.

The legislative process in the United States also mandates a majoritarian approach. Proposed legislation requires at least one more than half the votes in order to pass and a majority vote in committee before proposed legislation is forwarded to the full house for deliberation. In some circumstances, far more than a simple majority (50 percent + 1) is required, such as legislative overrides (two-thirds vote) and, where used, cloture votes (such as in the US Senate, which requires at least 60 percent for a cloture vote). The majoritarian characteristics of electoral and legislative systems render it difficult for minorities to become integrated into US politics. As SMD systems provide majority parties and voices with distinct advantages, it warrants our attention to consider Jewish women who have achieved electoral success and representation in legislatures that lack the advantages that majority status brings.

In 1994, the majority party in Congress and many state legislatures switched from Democratic to Republican. Several governorships did the same. Twelve years later, in 2006, the majority party in the US Congress switched back to Democratic dominance, although party dominance at the state level remained more Republican than Democratic. Despite recent Democratic successes, Democrats remain the minority party in many states where Jewish female Democratic legislators serve. The present study includes Jewish women elected 1990–2006. The year 1990 was chosen because it is two two-year election cycles before the start of the so-called Republican Revolution in 1994 (Edwards and Samples 2005). The year 2006 was chosen as the cutoff point because it signaled a decline in Republican Revolution gains due, in part, to the change in congressional party dominance that year.

Jewish female legislators represent an ideal, unexplored research population for understanding the roles that religious, gender, numeric, and sometimes partisan minorities play in a representative system structured around majoritarian principles. This study contributes to the growing work of scholars who focus on minority integration in legislatures and minority campaign strategies. These questions become more important as scholars and analysts consider the role that minorities play in electoral and legislative politics, and how their experiences impact representation in a democracy.

Citizenship studies are also enhanced by the work presented here. For example, Will Kymlicka, in his 1996 work *Multicultural Citizenship: A Liberal Theory of Minority Rights*, considers how modern societies reveal a "multicultural fabric" that brings with it new issues and conflicts, including, but not limited to, the status of minority cultures. Kymlicka investigates those issues that he considers critical to understanding multicultural politics, including group representation. Jewish women, as members of multiple minority groups, each of which represents a group that has sought political recognition, makes studying their participation in electoral and legislative politics helpful in understanding how liberal democracies respond to multicultural citizenship.

Earlier research on minorities in legislatures has focused on issues of gender (Swers 2002; Saint-Germain 1989), race (Barrett 1995), gender and race together (Barrett 2001), and political characteristics (Dotson 2001) using three approaches: intergroup comparisons (how members of different races or genders campaign for office or behave in a legislative context); intragroup analysis (how members of the same gender or race group behave within an electoral or legislative context); and case studies that take an in-depth look at individual legislators' governmental, political, electoral, and other pertinent experiences. The approach taken here is an intragroup analysis, where being Jewish, female, and elected constitutes the three criteria for study inclusion. An intragroup approach was taken because this approach would bear the most meaningful findings in light of the characteristics of the study population. Comparing Jewish and female state legislators to males, non-Jews, or both, would limit opportunities for generalizability. Both males and non-Jews represent meaningfully diverse populations such that drawing conclusions about each of these populations limits their value when making comparisons to Jewish women.

Focusing on how minorities function within majoritarian contexts helps one better understand how minorities become integrated into majority-focused political systems. Earlier studies that considered minority integration in majoritarian systems show that how one minority group functions within political systems, and minority group members' perceptions of that experience, is not generalizable to those attitudes and behaviors experienced by other minority groups. For example, African American women differ from African American men in their campaign and legislative behavior, as do African American women when compared with white women. One cannot assume how Jewish female legislators will behave in their campaign and legislative environments based on research studying other minority populations such as Protestant women or Catholics. Further, Jewish women constitute a unique identity-based minority that represents a much smaller percentage of the nation's population (1.5 percent) than do other minority groups that have successfully entered legislatures. Jewish women may face the same electoral and legislative hurdles as do other minorities, but do not experience them in the same way or to the same magnitude.

LITERATURE REVIEW

The research presented here builds on scholarship focusing on how minorities function within legislatures and the electoral conditions, tactics and strategies that minorities employ in their efforts to secure public office. Overall findings suggest that the manner that minorities campaign and function within legislatures differs from majority group members' experiences. Additionally, minorities are not monolithic in their legislative or campaign behavior: intragroup differences among minority groups linked to characteristics such as region, age, length of time in office, and political party membership impact minority behavior within legislatures and as candidates. These differences are attributed to minority legislators' backgrounds as members of previously discriminated-against groups as well as the political and structural consequences of long-term opposition to minority group members seeking and achieving political power.

Women as Gender Minorities in Legislatures

One widely cited study looks at how women function as gender and numerical minority group members in state legislatures. Sue Thomas found that women approach their legislative roles quite differently than male legislators. Her key question looks at the consequences of gender and numerical minorities in majoritarian, legislative contexts. Specifically, she asks whether women reform or adapt to their male dominated legislative environments. Thomas finds that women are more effective in passing woman-centered policies when there are more women working together on legislation (when women work together as members of the same party or caucus). She also finds that women are more effective at introducing and passing laws that take a feminist approach to public policy on issues concerning women, families, and children (Thomas 1994). A more recent study conducted by

Tracy Osborn modeled on Thomas's approach considered bills sponsored by women and found that political party plays an important role in women shaping policy alternatives addressing women's concerns. Still, Osborn, like Thomas, finds that women's legislative efforts focus meaningful attention on issues of particular concern to women (Osborn 2012).

Related to these efforts focusing on women in their legislative roles, Rosenthal considered how women function in legislative leadership roles (Rosenthal 1998, 2002). Rosenthal finds that female committee chairs exhibit leadership styles that differ from those leadership styles exhibited by male committee chairs. She further argues that female committee chairs use a more inclusive and collegial style compared with male committee chairs, an approach that leads to more topics being introduced and more committee members speaking in these small group settings. Such findings suggest that women reform, rather than adapt to, their legislative environments once a sufficiently large critical mass of women in those legislatures emerges (see also Thomas and Welch 2001; Rosenthal and Fox 2006). These findings also suggest that political processes and outcomes are affected by minority group status. As the minority group grows in size and stature, so too does that group's impact on political processes and outcomes.

More recently, Michelle Swers analyzed the political and policy behavior of women in the US Senate (Swers 2002). Like Thomas, Swers found that women in the Senate advocate for women's issues. Swers also found that political party and ideology impact the direction of female senators' policy approaches. While women more than men pursue social welfare and women's rights, party membership shapes how Democratic and Republican women approach these issues (Swers 2013).

Together, these studies from both state and federal levels find that female legislators behave differently than men in their legislative capacities. These studies also suggest that partisanship affects how women behave within legislatures and that women's effectiveness is impacted by the number of women in, and party control of, the legislature in which they serve.

Women as Racial and Gender Minorities in Legislatures

Racial group membership also impacts legislative behavior. Edith Barrett (1995, 2001), for example, found that African American female legislators were less likely to be married than their male counterparts. Further, both African American and white males tended to have entered politics younger than did women, which suggests that, by entering politics at an older age, one's political career is likely shorter. Barrett also found that African American legislators were more likely to be elected from areas with larger African American populations. On policy questions, Barrett found that African American women and men tended to be in greater agreement on issues of particular concern to African Americans, such as affirmative action, even though white women were more supportive of affirmative action than were white men. Similarly, Bratton, Haynie, and Reingold (2007) found that African American female state legislators focus attention on issues of particular interest to women and African Americans. At the same time, Bratton, Haynie, and Reingold suggest that African American women "are less likely to sponsor women's interest measures when a relatively high proportion of women is present in the legislature" (Bratton, Haynie, and Reingold 2007, 72).

The road to securing legislative seats is also affected by minority group membership. The public more often questions whether candidates meet the qualifications of the office being sought if they are minority group members due to factors that include stereotyping. Stereotyping occurs when voters impute traits and issue positions to a candidate based on beliefs about the characteristics associated with a group to which the candidate belongs (Dolan and Lynch 2014; see also Matson and Fine 2006). For example, Dolan (2010) found that support for female candidates declined as the level of office increased. Such reluctance among voters is often attributed to gender stereotypes about the type of person most suitable for office (Dolan and Sanbonmatsu 2009; Kennedy 2003; Dolan 2005; Fox and Oxley 2003) or the expectation that the direction of public policy will shift in a way that favors specific minority group members at the expense of majority groups should a member of that minority group be elected.

These studies find that gender and race, combined with numerical representation, individually and collectively impact legislative and electoral processes and legislative outcomes at the state and federal level. The factors explaining why minority group status affects one's political opportunities are often linked to socialized perceptions based on stereotypes (Dolan and Lynch 2014). In essence, the public, government, and linkage institutions needed for electoral success (political parties and interest groups) have questioned the qualifications, intent, and the likelihood of success of minority group members who are seeking elective office or pursuing a legislative agenda.

Women and the Electoral Environment

Minorities experience elections differently under diverse electoral and geographic environments. For example, Fulton considers whether voters view male and female candidates for the same office differently. Fulton suggests that a voter bias exists such that a sex-based quality gap is linked to electoral success to women's disadvantage (Fulton 2011). And women are also impacted by incumbency advantages in that women are more likely to lose when an incumbent is in the race because incumbents win and women are not usually incumbents (Carroll 1985; Welch and Studlar 1996). Similarly, Barrett (2001) found that African Americans are more likely to be elected from areas with higher percentages of African American residents than from those districts with low African American populations.

Ethnic voting also affects vote choice. McConnaughy and colleagues suggest that ethnic cues and ethnic appeals impact vote choice (McConnaughy et al. 2010; see also Rapoport, Metcalf, and Hartman 1989). McConnaughy and colleagues' findings reflect those indicated by Wolfinger (1965), who notes that voter ethnicity is associated with ethnic-based voting because of identification theory (see also Jones-Correa and Leal 2001). This theory suggests that voters prefer candidates of the same ethnicity, because members of that group hold favorable feelings about fellow members (Huddy 2001; Sigelman and Sigelman 1982).

Interest group endorsement and donation patterns show that certain groups are advantaged while others are less so. Incumbents tend to receive more donations, and donations of higher amounts, when compared to challengers, regardless of party (Fouirnaies and Hall 2014; see also Fine 1995), although groups formed for the specific purpose of electing members of minority groups (for example, EMILY's List[1] and the WISH List,[2] which were both formed to elect women) are working to minimize those patterns (Sanbonmatsu 2010). These research efforts demonstrate that minority status impacts legislative behavior and candidate experience.

Studying minorities in legislatures and as candidates is critical to understanding how democracies function. Jewish women compose an even smaller national population share than do other minorities who have won state-level legislative seats. This means that the more we know about Jewish women legislators, the better equipped we are to understand how minority groups succeed in majoritarian systems, and how citizenship is experienced through political representation in multicultural democracies.

DATA, METHODS, AND ANALYSIS

The first step in this process is identifying pertinent characteristics about Jewish female state legislators elected 1990–2006. Specific interest is directed toward questions about partisanship, states represented, individual and family characteristics, and prior political experience. In so doing, we will have a snapshot of the type of Jewish women who have succeeded in getting elected as members of multiple minority groups through majoritarian electoral processes and into majoritarian legislative contexts.

In total, forty-five women representing eighteen states were identified as having met the study criteria (Jewish, female, and elected to state legislative office between 1990 and 2006).[3] Of the eighteen states represented, New York and Florida constituted those with the highest representation of Jewish female legislators (nine and seven respectively), while eight states each had one Jewish female representative (see table 1) elected during this time. These findings indicate several patterns. For example, two of the three states with the highest Jewish populations also have the highest numbers of Jewish female state legislators (Florida and New York) among their state legislatures.[4] These data also show that Jewish female state legislators represent several "blue" states, where ideologically liberal candidates enjoy more electoral success than in other, more conservative "red" states.[5] The distribution of cases also shows, with few exceptions, a general pattern of bicoastal representation, where the Midwest and other central states, which have low Jewish population concentrations, and tend to be Republican-leaning, are not represented by Jewish females (see table 2). These findings also suggest that areas with higher Jewish populations are friendlier to electing Jewish representatives, including women. Alternately, the eligible candidate pool may have a higher percentage of Jewish candidates because the electoral district has a relatively higher proportion of Jewish residents.

Political and electoral experience is explored in the next section. The persons identified in this study follow typical political experience patterns. For instance, most elected women are Democrats, although the number of Republican women elected since the mid-1990s has increased. And Jews are predominately Democratic.[6] It would be reasonable to expect, then, that most Jewish female state legislators are Democrats. Here, the results show that thirty-nine of the forty-five women, or 87 percent, are Democrats.

Distribution between the two legislative chambers found in each state[7] shows that Jewish women holding state legislative seats are more likely to

Table 1. Jewish female state legislator distribution by state

State	Number of Legislators	Percent of Total
Arizona	2	4
California	3	7
Colorado	2	4
Connecticut	4	9
Florida	7	16
Illinois	4	9
Kansas	1	2
Kentucky	1	2
Michigan	2	4
North Carolina	1	2
New Hampshire	2	4
New Jersey	2	4
New York	9	20
Pennsylvania	1	2
Texas	1	2
Vermont	1	2
Washington	1	2
West Virginia	1	2
Total	45	97*

*Note: The small population size (45) contributes to the rounding error.

Table 2. Jewish female state legislator distribution by region*

Region	Number of Legislators	Percent of Total
Midwest	7	16
Northeast	19	42
South	11	24
West	8	18
Total	45	100

*Note: US Census regional divisions were used as the basis for determining these regions.

serve in their state House of Representatives (or parallel chamber) than in their state Senate. Of the forty-five women included in the study, 70 percent served in their state House (thirty-one), while 30 percent (fourteen) served in their state Senate from 1990 to 2006. Before being elected to their current

Table 3. Political background of Jewish female state legislators

Most Recent Office Served	Number of Legislators	Percent of Total
State House of Representatives (senators only)	12	27
County Commissioner	1	2
County Board of Education	4	9
City Board of Education	2	4
Mayor	1	2
City or Town Council	5	11
No Prior Elected Office	20	44
Total	45	99*

*Note: The small population size (45) contributes to the rounding error.

positions, these women served in a wide array of offices, including executive and legislative local government positions. Forty-five percent had held no prior office before being elected to their current position (see table 3), while twelve of the fourteen state senators (86 percent) had previously served as members of their state Houses.

The results show that a large share of these women served in some local level elective capacity before being elected to their state legislature. Nearly all state senators had served in their respective state Houses. These results also appear to follow a political career pattern women often exhibit, where political careers include those offices that cohere to stereotypical expectations of women. Diverse explanations outline why women are more likely to serve in lower-level elected offices, including stereotypes about women being better qualified to serve in local government than in state or national government, women have a better understanding of localized issues, such as education, or family dynamics where local and state offices do not preclude women from serving as family caretakers while holding public office. Here, six of the forty-five women had been elected as school board members, an office that voters often find is acceptable for women to hold because of gender stereotypes. It would be interesting to determine the percentage of all state legislative officials elected between 1990 and 2006 who had never served in public office before their first election to the legislature. This percentage could then be compared to the 45 percent of Jewish women who had never served in elected office before their election to the legislature to find out if 45 percent is higher or lower than the national average for all state legislators.

Table 4: Education level of Jewish female state legislators

Education Level	Number of Legislators	Percent of Total
High School	2	4
Associate Degree	1	2
College Degree	12	27
Graduate Degree (not Law)	14	31
Law Degree	13	30
Missing	3	6
Total	45	100

This percentage could also be compared to those who hold membership in specific cohorts such as Jewish men, all men, and all women.

The data presented here also show that these women represent the educational elite. Three-fourths of these women had a college degree or higher. This is typical for elected officials, who tend to have higher education levels than the population they represent.[8] Of all women included in the study, 33 percent (fourteen) had a master's degree, while 31 percent (thirteen) had earned a law degree (see table 4). In the general population, Jewish women tend to be better educated than are non-Jewish women (Sheskin 2004, 12). These results show that Jewish female state legislators' educational levels reflect those of the Jewish female population. At the same time, these data suggest that higher education represents an opportunity path for Jewish women seeking state legislative seats. This opportunity path may allay, in part, potential voter concerns about whether one can represent a district as a member of multiple minority groups that together compose a tiny population cohort. Put differently, voters may more likely support better educated candidates due to a perception that those candidates are better equipped to represent their district. Voters may perceive that Jewish women, most of whom have earned an advanced degree, may possess needed skills and tools to maneuver the legislative process as a result of their higher education. This approach suggests that Jewish women, whose education levels are higher, on average, than non-Jewish women, may be advantaged in their campaigns.

Additional information on family structure shows that most of these Jewish female legislators are married (73 percent), and more than 80 percent had at least one child. The average number of children was two; one legislator had five.

These results, taken together, suggest that Jewish female state legislators reflect trends among female legislators (local level experience achieved before seeking higher office), those of other minority populations (African American legislators tend to be more Democratic than Republican), and those of Jewish populations in the United States (higher education levels).

DISCUSSION AND CONCLUSION

The information presented here provides a snapshot of Jewish female state legislators elected 1990–2006. The findings suggest that Jewish female state legislators mirror other female state legislators in their overall partisan leanings and educational backgrounds, while Jewish women tend to represent those states where one finds the highest Jewish population concentrations. Jewish population concentration also suggests liberalism and Democratic leanings (Pew 2013). The results also indicate that most Jewish female state legislators served in the state House, while nearly half held no elected office before being elected to their current position. The results presented here also suggest that Jewish women state legislators reflect non-Jewish female state legislators in terms of political careers and family structure, while these results also indicate that these women differ from non-Jewish state legislators in terms of the extent of their partisan leanings. Jewish women are more heavily Democratic than are non-Jewish women (Pew 2015). The states where Jewish female state legislators are concentrated are those states that have higher Jewish population concentrations compared with those states with low Jewish population concentrations.

Future research will add to this study by analyzing electoral factors such as the conditions in which these women were elected to state government (for example, anecdotal reports suggest that many of these women unseated unpopular incumbents), the percentage of the vote they received in their election, issue positions, and interest group endorsement patterns. Prior research tells us that studying minorities in legislatures and as candidates is critical to understanding how democracies function, broadening our understanding of how a minority population that is small, and externally and internally identifiable, helps us better understand how minority groups function in majoritarian representative systems.

NOTES

1. EMILY stands for "Early Money Is Like Yeast (it makes the dough rise)." EMILY's List was formed in 1985 to elect Democratic, pro-choice female candidates to Congress.

2. WISH stands for "Women in the Senate and House." The WISH List was formed in 1992 to elect Republican, pro-choice female candidates to Congress.

3. Data collection was achieved through investigating multiple sources including LexisNexus (current Jewish female members of Congress who have previously served at the state level), Internet searches using appropriate search terms, the National Association of Jewish Legislators, Project Vote-Smart, www.politicalgraveyard.com, news archives, and Clerks of the House and Senate in each state (including state legislative directories), the Center for the American Woman in Politics (www.cawp.rutgers.edu), the *Almanac of State Legislatures State Data Atlas*, and the *Almanac of Women and Minorities in American Politics*.

4. The states with the largest Jewish populations in the United States are California, New York, and Florida; see Sheskin and Dashefsky (2012).

5. The categorization of "blue" representing predominately Democratic states and "red" representing predominately Republican states emerged in the 2000 presidential election season.

6. Jewish liberalism plays a key role in explaining Jewish Democratic party affiliation. See Wald (2015). See also Fine (1996).

7. Nebraska is the only state in the United States that has a unicameral legislature; there are no persons represented in this study who met the study criteria.

8. For example, in the 113th Congress (2015–17), 93 percent of the US House of Representatives and 99 percent of the Senate hold a bachelor's degree or higher while 29 percent of the US population holds a bachelor's degree or higher (US Census).

WORKS CITED

Barrett, Edith. 1995. "The Policy Priorities of African American Women in State Legislatures." *Legislative Studies Quarterly* 20 (2): 223–47.

———. 2001. "Black Women in State Legislatures: The Relationship of Race and Gender to the Legislative Experience." In *The Impact of Women in Public Office*, edited by Susan Carroll, 185–204. Bloomington: Indiana University Press.

Bratton, Kathleen, Kerry L. Haynie, and Beth Reingold. 2007. "Agenda Setting and African American Women in State Legislatures." In *Intersectionality and Politics: Recent Research on Gender, Race, and Representation in the United States*, edited by Carol Hardy-Fanta, 71–96. New York: Routledge.

Carroll, Susan. 2001. *The Impact of Women in Public Office*. Bloomington: Indiana University Press.

Dolan, Kathleen. 2005. "Do Women Candidates Play to Gender Stereotypes? Do Men Candidates Play to Women? Candidate Sex and Issues Priorities on Campaign Websites." *Political Research Quarterly* 58 (1): 31–44.

———. 2010. "The Impact of Gender Stereotyped Evaluations on Support for Women Candidates." *Political Behavior* 32 (1): 69–88.

———. 2014. "Gender Stereotypes, Candidate Evaluations, and Voting for Women Candidates: What Really Matters?" *Political Research Quarterly* 67 (1): 96–107.

Dolan, Kathleen, and Timothy Lynch. 2014. "It Takes a Survey: Understanding Gender Stereotypes, Abstract Attitudes, and Voting for Women Candidates." *American Politics Research* 42 (4): 656–76.

Dolan, Kathleen, and Kira Sanbonmatsu. 2009. "Gender Stereotypes and Attitudes toward Gender Balance in Government." *American Politics Research* 37 (3): 409–28.

Dotson, Debra L. 2001. "Acting for Women: Is What Legislators Say, What They Do?" In *The Impact of Women in Public Office*, edited by Susan Carroll, 225–42. Bloomington: Indiana University Press.

Edwards, Chris, and John Samples, eds. 2005. *The Republican Revolution 10 Years Later: Smaller Government or Business as Usual?* Washington, DC: Cato Institute, 2005.

Fine, Terri Susan. 1995. "Pro-Israel PAC Donation Patterns in Florida's 1992 Congressional Elections." Southern Political Science Association, Tampa, Florida.

———. 1996. "The Impact of Demographic and Social Change on the Jewish Political Agenda in the 1990s." In *The Politics of Minority Coalitions: Race, Ethnicity, and Shared Uncertainties*, edited by Wilbur C. Rich. Westport, CT: Greenwood Publishing.

Fouirnaies, Alexander, and Andrew Hall. 2014. "The Financial Incumbency Advantage: Causes and Consequences." *Journal of Politics* 76 (3): 711–24.

Fox, Richard L., and Zoe M. Oxley. 2003. "Gender Stereotyping in State Executive Elections: Candidate Selection and Success." *Journal of Politics* 65 (3): 833–50.

Fox, Richard L., and Eric R. A. N. Smith. 1988. "The Role of Candidate Sex in Voter Decision-Making." *Political Psychology* 19: 403–19.

Fulton, Sarah. 2011. "Running Backwards and in High Heels: The Gendered Quality Gap and Incumbent Electoral Success." *Political Research Quarterly* 65 (2): 303–14.

Hardy-Fanta, Carol, ed. 2007. *Intersectionality and Politics: Recent Research on Gender, Race, and Representation in the United States.* New York: Routledge.

Huddy, Leonie. 2001. "From Social to Political Identity: A Critical Examination of Social Identity Theory." *Political Psychology* 22: 127–56.

Jones-Correa, M., and D. Leal. 2001. "Political Participation: Does Religion Matter?" *Political Research Quarterly* 54 (4): 751–70.

Kennedy, Carole. 2003. "Gender Differences in Committee Decision-Making: Process and Outputs in an Experimental Setting. *Women and Politics* 25 (3): 27–45.

Kymlicka, Will. 1996. *Multicultural Citizenship: A Liberal Theory of Minority Rights.* Oxford: Clarendon Press.

Matson, Marsha, and Terri Fine. 2006. "Gender, Ethnicity, and Ballot Information: Ballot Cues in Low-Information Elections." *State Politics and Policy Quarterly* 6 (1): 49–72.

McConnaughy, Corrine M., Ismail K. White, David L. Leala, and Jason P. Casellasa. 2010. "A Latino on the Ballot: Explaining Coethnic Voting among Latinos and the Response of White Americans." *Journal of Politics* 72 (4): 1199–211.

Osborn, Tracy. 2012. *How Women Represent Women: Political Parties, Gender, and Representation in State Legislatures.* New York: Oxford University Press.

Pew Research Center. 2013. "A Portrait of Jewish Americans," chapter 6: "Social and Political Views," October 1.

———. 2015. "A Deep Dive into Party Affiliation," April 7.

Rapoport, Ronald B., Kelly L. Metcalf, and Jon A. Hartman. 1989. "Candidate Traits and Voter Inferences: An Experimental Study." *Journal of Politics* 51: 917–32.

Rich, Wilbur C. 1996. *The Politics of Minority Coalitions: Race, Ethnicity, and Shared Uncertainties.* Westport, CT: Greenwood Publishing, 1996.

Rosenthal, Cindy Simon. 1998. *When Women Lead: Integrative Leadership in State Legislatures.* New York: Oxford University Press.

———. 2000. "Gender Styles in State Legislative Committees Raising Their Voices in Resolving Conflict." *Women and Politics* 21 (2): 21–45.

Rosenthal, Cindy Simon, ed. 2002. *Women Transforming Congress.* Norman: University of Oklahoma Press.

Rosenthal, Cindy Simon, and Sarah J. Fox. 2006. "Observations about Congressional Leadership: Where Are the Women?" Paper presented at the Midwest Political Science Association annual meeting, Chicago, April 20–23.

Saint-Germain, Michelle. 1989. "Does Their Difference Make a Difference? The Impact of Women on Public Policy in the Arizona Legislature." *Social Science Quarterly* 70: 956–68.

Sanbonmatsu, Kira. 2010. "Life's a Party: Do Political Parties Help or Hinder Women?" *Harvard International Review* 32 (1): 36–39.

Sheskin, Ira. 2004. Geographic Differences among American Jews, Report #8, United Jewish Communities Report Series on the National Jewish Population Survey 2000–2001.

Sheskin, Ira M., and Arnold Dashefsky, eds. 2012. "Jewish Population in the United States, 2012." *American Jewish Year Book.* Dordrecht: Springer.

Sigelman, Lee, and Carol K. Sigelman. 1982. "Sexism, Racism and Ageism in Voting Behavior: An Experimental Analysis." *Social Psychology Quarterly* 45 (4): 263–69.

Swers, Michele. 2002. *The Difference Women Make: The Policy Impact of Women in Congress.* Chicago: University of Chicago Press.

———. 2013. *Women in the Club: Gender and Policy Making in the Senate.* Chicago: University of Chicago Press.

Thomas, Sue. 1994. *How Women Legislate.* New York: Oxford University Press.

Thomas, Sue, and Susan Welch. 2001. "The Impact of Women in State Legislatures: Numerical and Organizational Strength." In *The Impact of Women in Public Office*, edited by Susan Carroll, 166–83. Bloomington: Indiana University Press.

Wald, Kenneth. 2015. "The Choosing People: Interpreting the Puzzling Politics of American Jewry." *Politics and Religion* 8 (1): 4–35.

Welch, Susan, and Donley T. Studlar. 1996. "The Opportunity Structure for Women's Candidacies and Electability in Britain and the United States." *Political Research Quarterly* 49: 861–74.

Wolfinger, Raymond. 1965. "The Development and Persistence of Ethnic Voting." *American Political Science Review* 59 (4): 896–908.

5

ALIEN ENEMIES OR
NATURALIZED CITIZENS?

· · · · · · · · · ·

Representations of British-Born Residents
in the United States during the War of 1812

JOHN O'KEEFE

Joseph Warburton was executed on a Thursday. It was late in 1813, and his execution was intended as a warning to deserters from the Royal Navy, particularly those who had deserted and served with the United States Navy, as Warburton had done.[1]

But while the American and British navies had ceased fighting over his labor and body, American and British newspapers began to dispute accounts of Warburton's life and chosen allegiance. Had he "been brought to a sense of his crime" and "warned five other British seamen" as British papers claimed, or had he fled the brutal discipline of the British Navy and come to the United States, as American accounts counterclaimed? And was he a British subject by birth or had he tried to naturalize in the United States, only to be thwarted by the too-late passage of a law allowing alien enemies to naturalize if they had arrived prior to the start of hostilities? In the eyes of some the American public, Warburton's labor benefited the country, and in time he would have naturalized and officially, legally become the loyal American that he already was, a common view of many British alien enemies residing in the United States.

The debate about Warburton's intentions was not one that simply divided Americans from the British. During the first decade of the nineteenth century, debates had raged within the United States about the intentions of British subjects migrating into the country. Were they greedy merchants, conspiring to seize control of the fledgling American economy and make Americans utterly dependent on British manufactures? Or were they productive, hard-working new citizens of their adopted country? The debate, and with it, representations of British-born migrants, shaped popular discourse and government policy making. These representations of aliens and citizens of foreign birth profoundly affected not only the treatment of those migrants but also led to policy decisions and influenced the decision to enter into the war.

What I argue in this chapter is that the process of state surveillance and regulation of the citizen/alien divide both recategorized citizen and alien populations, based on existing representations of citizenship, while also being affected by the migrants' reactions themselves. The concept of the enemy during this war differed from other crises chiefly in that there was a shared sense of cultural (and racial) identity with the British Isles, so that the fierce debates over language or racial profiling that occurred in later conflicts were not at the government's disposal to sort out the seemingly dangerous from the peaceable. Historically, race and language served as the means by which the disloyal and others of suspect allegiance were identified, denationalized if not already, and stripped of legal and other rights. In contrast, other scholars have emphasized a limited trend toward the nationalization of citizenship prior to the Civil War. However, the War of 1812 functioned as a crucial test of the effectiveness of the early national government and its control over noncitizens. Similarly, while scholarship has emphasized the surveillance power of the nation-state in the twentieth century, compulsory registration of alien enemies was quite successful during the War of 1812, and perhaps more so than during World War I.[2]

Conversely, in dealing with the surveillance and deportations that were directed at them, British subjects chose to present themselves in specific ways to elicit the response they hoped to obtain from government officials. Many British subjects emphasized their peaceful nature and willingness to sit out the conflict, while others emphasized their intention to naturalize, or mentioned their American wives as surety of their friendliness to the US government. (The last of these functioned as an unwitting challenge to the Anglo-American legal tradition of coverture, whereby women's legal and civic identities were subsumed under their husbands or other male guardians.) British and Irish immigrants continued to rely on cultural markers rather than legal naturalization to defend their commitment to US citizenship, especially by emphasizing their incorporation into American households.

The period after US independence was a key point in the intersection of cultural ideas about citizenship and legal and political forms of citizenship as they developed in the nineteenth century. In writing new state constitutions as well as a new federal constitution, legislators transformed former colonial British subjects into American citizens, and with these new constitutions, needed to define, limit, and explain citizenship. Their cultural beliefs of who and who did not constitute members of American society, and who could exercise power in the political realm, meant that cultural ideas of citizenship informed, defined, and was separated by this early legislative process.

American citizenship law in the years before the War of 1812 reflected several key trends and struggles: the conflict between a liberal conception of citizenship that allowed the foreign-born to naturalize, and a nativist view that sought to exclude them. Political leaders who wanted to strengthen and centralize the national government also faced resistance from localists who favored a more decentralized system. The nationalists' most lasting success was the ratification of the United States Constitution, which contained a provision for a "uniform rule of naturalization." Congress passed such a law in 1790, which liberally granted the right to naturalize after two years but limited naturalization to whites only. Conflicts over race and gender also simmered after the American Revolution. Women and African Americans made limited gains in the early years but faced increasing limits on their civic participation after 1800.[3]

The other major conflict that affected citizenship was the emergence of the first party system in the United States. The Democratic-Republicans (often simply called Republicans, though different from today's Republican Party) was popular among artisans, yeoman farmers, and southern slave owners, and were more welcoming to most European immigrants. The Republican Party also saw common cause with revolutionary France. The Federalist Party counted among its supporters merchants, wealthy landowners, and New Englanders, and became increasingly hostile to European migrants during the 1790s, fearing the export of revolutionary views. Partisan conflict spilled into naturalization law in 1798, when the Federalist government passed a series of laws known as the Alien and Sedition Acts. The Sedition Act targeted defamatory publications aimed at Federalist leaders. The Naturalization Act of 1798 lengthened naturalization requirements to fourteen years of residence and instituted compulsory registration in federal courts for all white aliens. The Alien Act allowed the president to deport aliens he deemed dangerous, along with requiring incoming vessels to report alien arrivals. The Alien Enemies Act was also passed at this time, but did not come into force, as it only applied to cases where the United States declared war. However, the Alien Enemies Act contained provisions allowing for the detention and "removal" of aliens over fourteen years of age either via the federal courts or by federal marshals. These laws built on an existing distinction between citizens and noncitizens: noncitizens who bore allegiance to another sovereign state were aliens. Should the host state be in a state of war with another sovereign state, those aliens bearing allegiance to the hostile state fell into the category of alien enemies (Kettner 1978, 243–45).[4]

The War of 1812 was a key time during which the rights and privileges of citizenship expanded during a period of national emergency. Wartime citizenship transformed the polity and demanded a rescinding of the (often half-hearted) welcome given to foreign migrants, who now needed to be categorized, sorted, and evaluated for their loyalty to the new nation. To accomplish such a task, James Madison's Republican federal government put into force the then-dormant Alien Enemies Act of 1798. The enforcement of the Alien Enemies Act was a part of the growth of the modern American nation-state as it continued to decide who could and could not be a member of the polity.[5]

From a British perspective, the War of 1812 was a minor side conflict that erupted from the British government's attempts to secure control of sea trade and ensure naval dominance in the Napoleonic Wars. Both British and French forces wanted access to American grain and attempted to coerce American traders into their respective trading blocs. Additionally, the British Navy, short on manpower after twenty years of almost continual warfare, sought available men wherever it could and searched American merchant vessels for British men to man its ships. Citing rampant fraud, British officials often refused to recognize naturalized American citizens' claims that they had ceased to be British subjects—in fact, British law officially refused to recognize the expatriation of British subjects. British actions often left American merchant vessels short-staffed, and searches of vessels close to the American coast exacerbated tensions. Meanwhile, French officials occasionally seized American merchant vessels in retaliation for trading within the British bloc (Hickey 1989, 9–13, 17–20).

President Thomas Jefferson and his successor James Madison responded to British actions with a series of embargo measures of decreasing effectiveness. Both Jefferson and Madison realized that in practice, the United States was effectively drifting into the British trade system. Their economic and political philosophies cast such a relationship as a shameful dependence on Great Britain. In response, Republicans (also known as Democratic-Republicans, as mentioned previously) obtained passage of legislation that offered US participation in either the British or French trading blocs in exchange for a halt on the seizure of American merchant vessels. Several diplomatic disputes with Britain, coupled with a French acceptance of the American offer, pushed the United States further toward war with Britain. Madison obtained a Declaration of War from Congress, which he signed on June 18, 1812. The war would formally end in late 1814, though news of peace would not reach North America until early 1815 (Hickey 1989, 20–25, 44–46, 214).

In the meantime, concerns also arose about British subjects in the United States. In the years leading up to the war, British businesses had begun to send young men to American seaboard towns to manage exports. These men had begun to court young American women at the same time that they began to threaten local American businesses with cheaper British goods. Madison's administration began to see these men, and the British commercial dominance that they represented, as a danger to the nation (Hickey 1989, 9–13, 17–25, 4–46; Heaton 1951, 519–27, 520).

These fears also existed at the more local level, where Americans wondered about their British neighbors and their activities, even during the period leading up to the war. In a prelude to future concerns about the activities of the Masons, fraternal societies were often depicted as chief vectors of British intrigue and infiltration. In New Hampshire, the *Keene Sentinel*, a presumably Federalist paper, defended the inclusion of a British subject into a local "W. B. Society," explaining that although a British subject, he "came to this country when he was but *two* years of age," and that he was not yet twenty-one and ineligible to naturalize, but that he "intended to become an American citizen as soon as he became of age," and that failing to support "the *American form of Government"* would have prevented him from becoming a member. The announcement was also reprinted in the *Concord Gazette*. In other incidents, especially after the war began, Republican editors sought to cast aspersions on the Federalist-leaning Washington Society, which they alleged had been willing to admit dangerous aliens, including those who had been ordered away from the coast, and former loyalists who had *"fought against Washington* in the [R]evolutionary [W]ar." Many of the inhabitants remembered the divisions of the revolution and knew who among their neighbors had been Loyalists, and those former Loyalists who remained would face increasing suspicion as the country geared up for war with Britain.[6]

Once the war began, other papers examined existing alien laws, and several papers noted that while the laws of the Alien and Sedition Acts had for the most part expired, the Alien Enemies Act of 1798 remained in force. Moreover, they also noted that existing laws forbade a change of allegiance in wartime. One paper to comment extensively on the laws saw them as necessary to prevent British infiltration of the country:

> The time has arrived when the president may exercise the authorities vested in him by the act of '98 . . . and we trust that a system of police will be carried into execution, which is demanded by the quantity of British influence in this country, and without which spies may flock in upon us to watch our movements and blast our enterprises. When British officers themselves steal in disguise among us, it is time to arrest the evil. A system is apparently required of a similar nature with the British *alien office*; a system, which shall grant licenses for residence, *passports* for travel, and warrants for removal. We feel the importance of the subject, and we invited the attention of the constituted authorities of the nation to it.[7]

Such was the concern in Madison's administration that several days after the declaration of war (and before the republication of the above article in the New York *Columbian*), the State Department issued orders to federal marshals requiring all alien enemies to register themselves or face deportation, stating as follows:

> All British subjects within the United States are required forthwith to report to the marshals (or to the persons appointed by them)

of the respective states or territories within which they may reside, their names, their age, the time they have been in the United States, the persons composing their families, the places of their residence, and their occupational pursuits, and whether, at what time, they have made the application to the courts required by law, as preparatory to their naturalization; and the marshals, respectively, are to make to the Department of State returns of all such British subjects, with the above circumstances attached to their names. (Lockington, Tilghman, and Bache 1813, appendix iii–iv)[8]

For the time being, the Madison administration deemed such measures sufficient, and federal marshals began to publish newspaper notices in July of 1812 informing aliens that they needed to register. Unlike similar provisions in the 1798 Alien Friends Act, these measures began to be enforced, including in areas of strong opposition to the war, such as Massachusetts, whose federal marshals collected the most detailed information of all state returns of alien enemies. Emphasizing the danger of a possible merchant cabal, the State Department followed the earlier orders with a February 23, 1813, removal order for all alien enemies involved in commerce (Lockington, Tilghman, and Bache 1813, iv–v):[9]

Alien enemies, residing or being within forty miles of tide water, are required forthwith to apply to the marshals of the states or territories in which they respectively are, for passports to retire to such places, beyond that distance from tide water, as may be designated by the marshals. This regulation, however, is not to be put in force without special notice against such alien enemies, not engaged in commerce, as were settled previously to the declaration of war in their present abode, or are there pursuing some regular and lawful occupation, unconnected with commerce, and who obtain monthly, from the marshal of the district in which they reside, permission to remain where they are. (Lockington, Tilghman, and Bache 1813, v)

The proclamation's language is somewhat convoluted, but it places alien enemies into three categories: those whom Madison administration officials wished to keep rooted in one place so that they could continue contributing to the agricultural and manufacturing sectors of the economy and whose activities would continue to be monitored; and a second, more dangerous class, those "engaged in commerce," as well as a third class of migrants without "regular and lawful occupation." In making this distinction, Madison's government was drawing on a long-standing difference between Federalists and Republicans. Republicans revered the farmer and the artisan as ideal citizens, while they regarded merchants with suspicion. Federalists, by contrast, were much more sympathetic to merchants as key participants in building a strong nation.

The government's surveillance, by concentrating on male heads of household, confined itself to the public sphere. The returns contain information about British subjects that were a matter of public record and public presentation, rather than information from within the household, other than the number of dependents. Except for the marshal of Massachusetts, all marshals forwarded returns that listed wives and children only by number, occasionally also including the number of servants or boarders ("inmates") in the household. Comments regarding suspicious individuals were confined to the head of household—dependents were assumed to be incapable of acting independently of the head of household.[10]

Despite the potential for highlighting Republican high-handedness, Federalists generally accepted the alien policies of the Madison administration. Federalists only made a public issue of one prominent deportee, George K. Jackson, representing him as a harmless music teacher who had been expelled from Boston per the removal order. Although a few aliens were granted indulgence, Jackson does not appear on the list of those granted; instead, Dr. "Jackson, of Boston" is listed as "removed to interior." Jackson's passport indicates that he was "ordered to Northampton, Hampshire Co.," in the interior of Massachusetts. The Boston *Daily Advertiser*, in describing a concert in honor of Russian victories over France, stated that the "the ill-timed exercise of the despotic power of the executive . . . deprived the public of the services of Dr. Jackson," and strongly hinted that the cause was "the malice of party feelings."[11]

The existing cultural and legal association in which aliens were persons of concern, and who was and was not a citizen, served to reinforce those claims by virtue of their reproduction—In other words, when government officials decided they needed to gather information about certain types of suspect individuals and assign a citizen or alien status to those individuals, government officials created and reinforced the criteria for deciding who was suspect, who was a citizen, and who was an alien, especially when producing documents for other government officials, who reiterated the process. The returns produced a representation of a typical British subject in the minds of State and War Department officials who were responsible for determining the legal categories of citizen and alien. This was especially true for former Loyalists and their children, who, if they continued to associate themselves with the Federalist Party and opposition to the war, were sometimes classified as aliens by government officials and listed in the alien returns. Association with the Federalist Party, receipt of pensions of half-pay retired status from British armed forces, or an outright rejection of US citizenship could all contribute to alien status, but former Loyalists who kept a low profile or demonstrated their newfound patriotism could find their US citizenship status affirmed. Among those who chose to behave otherwise and consequently draw the attention of the national government was John C. Gray, who was born in Halifax to Loyalist parents originally from Massachusetts. The family resettled in Boston in 1790, and John Gray established himself as a printer in Danbury, Connecticut, where he published the *Connecticut Intelligencer.* Gray's Federalist partisanship was cause for suspicion about his true motives and citizenship status. Gray "claim[ed] to be a citizen of the U.S." and "sa[id] he had bee[n] admitted to the right of suffrage in Mass and Connect for 10 years past," but the collector of returns for Danbury thought it necessary to include him among the returns, noting that "Since he came into this State (about 5 years ago) he has been a tool of the federal party, to print a newspaper full of abuse & falsehood agt the govt of U.S." The report showed the existing partisan divide and the tensions that heightened it during the war as New Englanders opposed it and began to consider secession as an option. However, Gray's more middling class status as a printer exempted him from being painted as a foreign infiltrator. Rather, he was depicted as someone being manipulated by the Federalist elite. The report also showed the continuing tension between state citizenship and citizenship at the national, federal level, while affirming the growing connection between citizenship and suffrage. The reporter, skeptical of Gray's federal status, separated his claims to state suffrage from US citizenship.[12]

Although those who had retired from the British armed forces were subject to scrutiny as civilians, the armed forces was a site where representations of citizenship and alienship were especially publicly contested. British-born sailors who enlisted in the US Navy were a key point of public concern.

As mentioned in the introduction of this chapter, mariner Joseph Warburton, who had immigrated to the United States and according to newspaper reports declared his intent to naturalize, served aboard the USS *Chesapeake* and was executed "for being found in arms against his country" of birth. Initial reports came copied from English newspapers that reported that Warburton "had been brought to sense of his crime" and "acknowledged the propriety of the sentence that awaited him," while warning five other British-born seamen from the *Chesapeake* to "never be wanting in feelings of fidelity for their King and Country." However, the *Essex Register* countered with additional details of Warburton's life, stating that he left the navy when his last voyage suffered from dangerous storms and a drunken prize master, causing the crew to "put themselves under the protection of the original captain," and then working as a crewmember for a number of other ships. The *Essex Register* also claimed that Warburton was a "remarkably intelligent and well educated young man," and further noted that after five years' residence in the United States, Warburton "applied to an attorney to be naturalized, but war having been declared, and the additional act of Congress not having passed [allowing wartime naturalizations of alien enemies], he could not effect his wishes," further claiming that he had wished to naturalize ever since his arrival in the United States. Thus while English (and some American) newspapers portrayed Warburton as a prodigal son who accepted the fitness of his punishment, other American papers presented him as a victim of the excesses of the British Navy, while serving his adopted country, and attempting to formalize his status as a citizen.[13]

Irish immigrants sometimes saw the war as a struggle against British (or English) power, and publicly projected an image of a joint Irish-American identity unified by the war. Irish immigration from 1783 to 1812 has been estimated at about 150,000, about two-thirds of whom were Presbyterians from the north, and the others a mixture of Anglicans and Catholics from the rest of the island. Among these were a number of political refugees from the failed 1798 rebellion. Despite significant Protestant-Catholic tension in Ireland, the 1798 rebellion, led by the United Irishmen, attempted to unite discontented Irish Catholics and Protestants against British rule. Many of its leaders, along with political dissidents from England such as Joseph Priestley, immigrated to the United States during the 1790s. However, they were part of a broader stream of migrants leaving the British Isles for economic reasons. Irish emigrants active in public life, such as Thomas Addis Emmet or John Binns, often had pasts associated with the United Irishmen or other radical movements, and publicly were hostile to Great Britain (Durey 1997, 1–5; Miller 1985, 169–73).

These Irish immigrants had access to emerging ethnic newspapers targeted at them. New York–based publications such as the *Shamrock* and the *Western Star* (or *Harp of Erin*) mainly carried articles concerning Irish politics and Anglo-Irish relations, although Philadelphia lacked such an ethnic press in the early nineteenth century. However, these papers provided information to their audiences about US government policies regarding them, as they fell under the category of alien enemies during the War of 1812, but coverage tended to avoid direct challenges to Irish emigrants' status as alien enemies, tending toward informing Irish emigrants of their legal rights and (dis)abilities. The *Shamrock* began its coverage with a reprint of a legal commentary, which had originally appeared in the Savannah *Republican*. The commentary stated that under international law ("the law of nations") allegiance could not be transferred from one sovereign or state to another in time of war. The opinion stated that regardless of whether the required maximum residency of five years had been fulfilled, applications to naturalize could not be admitted. In the fall, the *Shamrock* published an article titled "Informations to Aliens," which summarized the regulations in force regarding British subjects, noting that "a large majority of [emigrants] . . . are unacquainted with our laws respecting them." The article summarized the order requiring alien enemies to register with US marshals and also noted that the provisions of the Alien Enemies Act of 1798 remained in force, and that state and federal courts had the right to deport British subjects, or require "securities for their good behavior." The article then summarized the regulations of the Naturalization Act of 1802, emphasizing the residency requirements, the necessity of the declaration of intent to naturalize at least two years prior to the petition to naturalize, and lastly noting that although the state of war prohibited naturalization, "aliens are not . . . prohibited from filing the declaration of their intention to become citizens."[14]

Among these was a poem that appeared in the New York *Shamrock* reprinted from the Petersburg *Republican*. The poem urged Americans to fight patriotically in the war, imploring: "Let each free-born Columbian rise, / And her adopted sons likewise, / And guard your hallow'd shore." The poem further went on to excoriate those reluctant to fight, "Or any base-born fiend of hell, / Whom British gold could tempt to sell, / His country's cause, or friend." The poem was signed "AN IRISH ALIEN," contrasting the author's patriotic zeal for his country of residence with his legal status as an alien enemy. Consistent with the paper's main focus on Anglo-Irish relations, the *Shamrock* followed with another poem below the first, originally printed in the Dublin *Anti-Union*, which compared the relationship between England and Ireland as that between two ships traveling together in rough and dangerous seas, one of whose crews expressed mutinous feelings. The *Shamrock* introduced the poem, noting its thinly veiled allegory, and added that "there exists a strong probability that a fortunate broadside from an American 'non-descript,' may release the captive, and permit her to sail on her own account and risque."[15]

In addition to poetry, the *Shamrock* also published longer prose essays, which appear to be original compositions. A rambling postwar essay that also addressed such topics as the liberty of the "savage of the wilderness" and advocated for more internal improvements in the United States began with an emphasis on the author's loyalty to the United States, stating: "America is my country, to it I owe allegiance, it is the birthplace of my children, and the home of many of my connexions." The author emphasized that this allegiance was due to American "liberty" and "happiness." He contrasted this state with the growing distance he felt from those he knew in Ireland, stating that they had "been sliding into another world." For the author, it was not just common cause with the United States in the recent war but also an American willingness to include its white men fully into the polity, even should the author's "means be more limited than those of my fellow citizens."[16]

This patriotic zeal obscures the existence of a population that may have had more mixed feelings toward the war, especially among Irish emigrants of more Unionist sympathies—although later in the nineteenth century, Unionism became linked to Irish Protestants, the 1801 Act of Union had initially been greeted optimistically by many Irish Catholics as a step toward political enfranchisement, and Irish American Catholics may have felt similarly. Still other Irish migrants may have felt rather indifferent to the United States and the war, having migrated for economic reasons and perhaps intending to return to Ireland with savings and purchase land or otherwise make use of their American earnings.

These feelings are illustrated most clearly in a series of letters written by Mary Craig Cumming, who left her native town of Lisburne, near Belfast, and settled in Petersburg, Virginia, with her husband. During the war, Mary

Cumming was able to send letters to her family in Ireland via prisoner exchange ships. Since they were not subject to the removal order and did not leave Petersburg, her husband must have obtained US citizenship. She herself was surprised by the declaration of war, writing that although her "Father's fears are now realized," Mary "could never bring myself to believe that [Great Britain and the United States] would go to war." Mary Cumming did not care for "Jimmy Madison," but she found the topic difficult to avoid in Petersburg society, as she wrote to her father:[17]

> Men, women, and children are all politicians in this country, politics is the general topic of conversation among the gentlemen and even of the ladies of this place. Some of the females of my acquaintance are most violent democrats. I say nothing, but I assure you I do not feel pleasant when I hear old England spoken of disrespectfully. . . . After all, I see no people so happy nor no government so good as my own. They talk of this being a land of liberty and such stuff, but in my opinion it is not so much so as Great Britain.[18]

Thus Mary, regardless of her status as a US citizen, retained considerable sympathies with Great Britain during the war—she was certainly no United Irishwoman, closing her letter with an expression of praise for the British government's treatment of its subjects. Nonetheless, her letters frequently express a frustration that the war had prevented her and her husband's planned return to Ireland. What she wanted most of all was peace, which she declared "the most wonderful news" once news of it finally arrived in 1815. Legally, under the doctrine of coverture, Mary Cumming was a US citizen. But she did not view herself as an American, even if the law stated that she was—Cumming in some ways was the opposite of the American wives of British men, who Americanized their husbands even if under the law they were British subjects.[19]

Other associates of the Cummings had a different, and more violent, experience during the war. Cumming happened to be traveling through Baltimore at the time of the Battle of Fort McHenry and was staying with the family of banker Alexander Brown. Brown had been a linen merchant but had since become involved in banking and organized the Baltimore Water Company in 1804. He was, in other words, heavily invested in the local community. According to Cumming, "Mr. Brown's family went into the country till the alarm had subsided," which meant his country estate, Springfield, not far from present-day Johns Hopkins Hospital. However, "two of his sons" remained in the city to assist in its defense in the event that British forces returned. The Brown family differed from the Cummings in committing itself more firmly to the American cause, regardless of whatever personal reservations Alexander Brown himself may have had. In a town where men of vocal antiwar leanings could find themselves subject to vigilante rioting, perhaps it was better to enroll one's sons in the armed forces even if they truly felt a stronger allegiance to Great Britain.[20]

Despite a growing nationalization of citizenship, and increasing national governmental authority over the categorization of citizens and aliens, aliens themselves also displayed alternative understandings of citizenship. Aliens noted in their returns the ways in which, although legally alien, they were not truly foreign. One of the most important ways that they might become cultural citizens was through the household. Some men argued that their apprenticeships served to incorporate them into American households, and thus, automatically naturalize them. William Young, a "Carver & Gilder" residing in Philadelphia, stated that "he served 9 Years apprenticeship in the City of New York & that he was informed that [coming into] the country while a minor & serving an apprenticeship was sufficient to entitle him to the privileges of a citizen." Two wire-workers and a "Printer & Glazier" also noted their apprenticeships but did not explicitly claim citizenship.[21]

Although the above understanding of apprenticeship indicates a continuation of the understanding of the implicitly male head of household conferring his legal status on all his dependents, some respondents differed from this pattern by indicating their marriages to American women. Robert Dunn, of Philadelphia, noted that he was "married to an American Lady." William Nottingham also mentioned his marriage to "a Lady a native of New Jersey Daughter of a Revolutionary Officer." In emphasizing how their American-born wives had Americanized them, they subtly undermined the legal tradition of coverture, wherein a husband legally covered his wife from presence in the public, legal sphere. The choice of description of these women as ladies indicates a successful deployment of Republican motherhood into Republican wifehood—their elite status and family prominence could serve to republicanize and Americanize their foreign-born husbands. Officials concurred with these claims, exempting men "married to natives" from the aforementioned removal order—on this claim, the British aliens won. While there might have been misgivings about British men marrying American women that circulated in the years before the war, the government accepted their participation in a normative marriage as a cultural marker of citizenship that assuaged concerns about loyalty, and, to some degree, incorporated those households in the American nation.[22]

Still other aliens, especially those required to move from coastal areas, argued that their peaceable nature and status as private citizens should exempt them from the removal order. Mrs. Balfour Thompson, who ran a shop in Richmond, Virginia, with her brother-in-law, wrote asking for an exemption for him, stating that her brother-in-law "never spoke disrespectfully of the Government," and that without him, she would be unable to find anyone "that would understand the store business for me." Navy supplier Hugh Scott wrote from Suffolk, stating "I have never interfered or taken part in the disputes of Political Parties, my Crime is being born in a foreign country, although my Interests & affections are here," hoping to be allowed to return to Norfolk and attend to his business, despite his arrest in Suffolk, Virginia, for violation of the order. Overall, marshals' returns and letters written emphasize aliens' good standing in their communities, and "friendliness to the government of the United States," attempting to extricate private persons from affairs of state and orders that threatened to destroy their economic livelihoods.[23]

American representations of British subjects appeared through the lens of mercantilism: British residents were either economically productive citizens or potential citizens (like the aforementioned Joseph Warburton), or part of a cabal of evil merchants plotting to seize control of the American economy. These views drove wartime policy and treatment of aliens, particularly for former Loyalists and their children. Furthermore, officials' insistence on viewing the implicitly male head of household attempted to keep citizenship, and with it, political agency, attached to the head of household. Nonetheless, changing ideas, at least concerning elite women, were undermining this view. Aliens were capable of influencing the categorization of households by drawing on American conceptions of how a household and its members could be Americanized culturally and therefore politically, though this transformation tended to be limited to genteel binational households, while former apprentices were less successful at changing or influencing categories of citizenship.

The responses of migrants were given under pressure to end the regime of surveillance and removal that the federal government had successfully put into place for the first time. Writers to government officials, hoping to be exempted from removal, sought to emphasize their peaceable natures and friendliness to the government.

The representations of citizenship and their effects upon government policy making would have important consequences for the future of American citizenship, as well as importance for rights and state power in times of international conflict. The crisis of the War of 1812 confirmed national power over citizenship in times of emergency, at the expense of local or state citizenship. The national government forcibly moved residents who had fallen into the category of potential political threats. The accrual of national power happened with local cooperation, rather than through local opposition. Surveillance effectively mobilized local citizens to create a centralized database of British subjects whom the federal government could target for forced removal. This power was concentrated in the executive branch of government, rather than the judiciary, which had played a much larger role in the 1790s, and power over foreign migrants would continue to accrue during periodic national crises such as the two world wars and the War on Terror. The consequences were difficult for many British subjects, but would prove disastrous in further national crises where groups, whose native-born citizens were often designated "forever foreign," most notably in the internment of Japanese Americans in World War II.

NOTES

1. *New York Columbian*, March 22, 1814; *Essex Register*, March 23, 1814; *New-England Palladium*, March 29, 1814.

2. In examining other early Republican citizenship trends, Kettner (1978, 249–51) has noted the ongoing federalization of citizenship during the early republican and antebellum periods, when legal authority to regulate the categories of citizenship increasingly drifted toward the national level of government. This article, in studying the growth of federal surveillance during the wartime emergency, places Kettner's work in concert with that of Zolberg (2006, 11–15), who noted that government regulation of naturalization and migration was part of the ongoing emergence of the modern nation-state. I also use Glenn's (2002, 54) model of facets of citizenship (standing, nationality, allegiance) as the means by which legal rights were accorded to citizens.

Capozzola (2008, 173, 204) also notes the continued use of the alien enemies act during World War I, noting that after the cessation of hostilities, the law was used to detain and deport immigrants of suspected revolutionary sympathies from the United States. Capozzola also notes the relative ineffectiveness of attempts to register German aliens during World War I. The fears of radicals were presaged by existing fears of German acts of terrorism, sabotage, and espionage discussed by Kazal (2004). In examining the responses of interned Japanese Americans during World War II, Collins (1985, 84–85) argues that the renunciation of citizenship by over five thousand Japanese Americans, or approximately 7 percent the total Japanese American population of the United States, was the result of an atmosphere of panic and uncertainty among interned Japanese Americans, who felt threatened not only by official surveillance and internment and the threat of further actions such as drafting into the US armed forces, but also by a growing and at times violent resistance movement within the internment camps, further complicated by failure on the part of US officials to understand the ways in which interned Japanese Americans felt threatened and their narrow interpretation of (de)naturalization law. Similarly, Capozzola, in examining the conflicting loyalties that German Americans in World War I encountered, argues that as alien enemies the easiest path for most German Americans was a public silence concerning their wartime attitudes and allegiance, and that this silence damaged existing German immigrant cultural institutions in which participation was deemed by nativists as suspect (Capozzola 2008, 176).

3. US Const. art. I, § 8, cl. 4. *Statutes at Large*, I, 103. Difficulties women and African Americans faced are discussed in Zagarri (2007), and Bradburn (2009, 235–71). Additionally, federal policies during the War of 1812 reinforced a view of citizenship being a status attached to the implicitly white and male head of household, excepting the possible subversions of coverture discussed elsewhere in this essay. In general, government officials concentrated their surveillance on the head of household and seem not to have been concerned about the possible activities of wives, children, servants, or enslaved people. This attitude did run alongside a US push to secure the return of enslaved African Americans who had been offered (and received) freedom by British forces.

4. See also *Statutes at Large*, I, 566–72, 577–78, 596–97. Some, but not all of these provisions were superseded by the Naturalization Acts of 1802 and 1805.

5. Between 1798 and 1800, the United States fought an undeclared war with France, the Quasi-War. Because the Quasi-War remained an undeclared war, the provisions of the Alien Enemies Act never came into force in the 1790s. Although the Republican-controlled Congress did not repeal the act, they had not forgotten about it—and in fact passed a supplementary act

on July 6, 1812, less than a month after the start of the War of 1812. The act stated that "nothing in the . . . [Alien Enemies Act] shall be extended or construed to extend to any treaty, or to any article of any treaty, which shall have expired, or which shall not be in force, at the time when the Proclamation of the President shall issue." *US Statutes at Large* 2 (1850): 781. This legislation presumably would allow the Madison administration a free hand in issuing orders regarding alien enemies.

6. *Concord Gazette*, May 26, 1812, 3. Originally printed in *Keene Sentinel*. *New-Jersey Journal*, May 3, 1814, 2. "W. B. Society" is probably the Washington Benevolent Society.

7. *New York Columbian*, July 13, 1812, 3. Reprint from the *Enquirer*. Italics original.

8. This order came after the end of the congressional session, so the Madison administration may have waited either for Congress to pass legislation like this, or to avoid Federalist objections during the session, and simply have the order be a fait accompli once Congress reconvened in November. In *Lockington v. Smith*, Charles Lockington, a British subject, violated the removal order, returned to Philadelphia, and was arrested and confined in the debtor's apartment by the federal marshal for Pennsylvania. Lockington sued in state court, petitioning for a writ of habeas corpus, and the Supreme Court of Pennsylvania ruled that it did not have jurisdiction.

9. Marshals' Returns of Enemy Aliens and Prisoners of War, 1812–1815, National Archives Record Group 59: General Records of the Department of State, 1756–1999, microfilm publication M588: "War of 1812 Papers" of the Department of State 1789–1815. Marshals' returns have been compiled, excepting original "remarks" field, in Scott (1979). Further marshals' returns of enemy aliens will be referred to by name, e.g., "return of firstname lastname." Some discussion of the compulsory alien registration and forced removal can be found in Henderson (1985, 99–110).

10. The motivations for more extensive record keeping in Massachusetts are unclear. This could be a result of continuing viewing other members of the household as politically independent, or looking for data within the household indicating an Americanizing presence, a willingness to be more intrusive than in other states, following local census-taking practices, or personal choice of the US marshal in Massachusetts.

11. Petition of Charles Lockington the Supreme Court of Pennsylvania. *New York Herald*, January 15, 1814, 4. Note that the original petition is not included in Lockington, Tilghman, and Bache (1813). Return of Job Fawke,

July 21, 1812. In *British Aliens in the United States*, Scott (1979) has transcribed Jackson's passport as follows: Jackson, George K. age 34, 5 ft. 4 1/2 in., florid complex., dark hair, blue eyes, prof. of music, Boston, on 19 Mar. 1812 ordered to Northampton, Hampshire Co. (Mass. Passport No. 3.)" However, the removal probably dates to 1813, as war had not yet been declared in 1812 (Scott 1979, 384). "Solemnities and Festival in Honor of the Russians," *Georgetown Federal Republican*, April 7, 1813, 1. Some discussion of Jackson appears in Johnson (1943b, x, 211), as well as Johnson (1943a, 113–21).

12. Return of John C. Gray (transcribed as "Grey" in Scott [1979]), August 16– September 26, 1812. Thomas et al. (1874, 297).

13. *New England Palladium*, March 23, 1814, 1; *New York Columbian*, March 22, 1814, 2. English account of Warburton's execution also appeared in *Danbury Gazette*, March 29, 3, and *Connecticut Mirror*, April 4, 2. *Essex Register*, March 23, 1814, 1. American accounts also appeared the *New England Palladium*, March 29, 1; *New Hampshire Patriot* (Concord) April 5, 3; *Alexandria Gazette Commercial and Political*, April 9, 3; *Farmers Repository* (Charlestown, West Virginia), April 21, 3.

14. *Shamrock*, August 1, 1812, 1; November 14, 1812, 4. The commentary was either by court clerk Job F. Belles or solicitor general Thomas U. P. Charlton. "Information to Aliens" at no time specifically states that the article pertains to Irish people or British subjects generally.

15. *Shamrock*, April 17, 1813, 4.

16. *Shamrock*, January 6, 1816, 116–17. In *Transatlantic Radicals*, Durey notes (1997, 331n1) that *Shamrock* editor Edward Gillespy emphasized the mercantile argument that immigrants were a benefit to the United States.

17. Letter of Mary Craig Cumming, December 20, 1813, note 1, March 9, 1814; Mary Cumming to Margaret Craig, June 24, 1812; December 20, 1813, in Irvine (1982).

18. Mary Cumming to Andrew Craig, December 20, 1813. Also, in letter dated January 2, 1814: "I believe in my soul many Americans wish old England was sunk in the sea, but she will flourish great and free, the dread and envy of them all."

19. Mary Cumming to Margaret Craig, February 9, 1815. Unfortunately for Mary, she was suffering from a severe illness that would result in her death two months later; Mary Cumming to Andrew Craig, October 14, 1814.

20. Mary Cumming to Andrew Craig, October 14, 1814.

21. Return of William Young, July 24, 1812; William Lancaster Jr., July 20, 1812; William Plews, July 20, 1812.

22. Return of Robert Dunn, July 20, 1812; William Nottingham, July 22, 1812. Letter of James Mercer to John Minor, March 31, 1813. Lockington, Tilghman, and Bache (1813), appendix vi.
23. Letters of Mrs. Balfour Thompson, March 20, 1813, and Hugh Scott, September 11, 1813, Letters Received Regarding Enemy Aliens, M588, War of 1812 Papers. British subjects' claims were also countered in an anonymous letter by "N. F." of Richmond, Virginia, dated March 16, 1813, arguing against indulgence:

> Many of these very applicants have had it in their power to have taken the Oath long ago and have been heard to say they would never forsake their King and County etc.
>
> One of the applicants for whom there is the greatest exertion made is a man who has violated the Embargo and would ruin the Country to aid the detestable British. My opinion is that there should be no favour granted any one at all and let each share the same fate. . . . I hope . . . for your own and for our much injured Country, and our Republican cause that, you will set your face against all application of that sort.
>
> Our Marshall I fear is doing very wrong in giving permissions for any alien to remain under any circumstances.

WORKS CITED

Bradburn, Douglas. 2009. *The Citizenship Revolution: Politics and the Creation of the American Union, 1774–1804*. Charlottesville: University of Virginia Press.

Capozzola, Christopher. 2008. *Uncle Sam Wants You: World War I and the Making of the Modern American Citizen*. Oxford: Oxford University Press.

Collins, Donald E. 1985. *Native American Aliens: Disloyalty and the Renunciation of Citizenship by Japanese Americans during World War II*. Westport, CT: Greenwood Press.

Durey, Michael. 1997. *Transatlantic Radicals and the Early American Republic*. Lawrence: University Press of Kansas.

Glenn, Evelyn Nakano. 2002. *Unequal Freedom: How Race and Gender Shaped American Citizenship and Labor*. Cambridge, MA: Harvard University Press.

Heaton, Herbert. 1951. "The Industrial Immigrant in the United States, 1783–1812." Proceedings of the American Philosophical Society 95.

Henderson, Dwight F. 1985. *Congress, Courts, and Criminals: The Development of Federal Criminal Law, 1801–1829*. Westport, CT: Greenwood Press.

Hickey, Donald R. 1989. *The War of 1812: A Forgotten Conflict*. Urbana: University of Illinois Press.

Irvine, Jimmy, ed. 1982. *Mary Cumming's Letters Home to Lisburn from America, 1811–1815*. Coleraine, Northern Ireland: Impact-Amergin.

Johnson, Harold Earle. 1943a. "George K. Jackson, Doctor of Music." *Musical Quarterly* 29 (1): 113–21.

———. 1943b. *Musical Interludes in Boston*. New York: Columbia University Press.

Kazal Russell A. 2004. *Becoming Old Stock: The Paradox of German-American Identity*. Princeton, NJ: Princeton University Press.

Kettner James. 1978. *The Development of American Citizenship, 1608–1870*. Chapel Hill: University of North Carolina Press.

Lockington, Charles, William Tilghman, and Richard Bache. 1813. *The Case of Alien Enemies, Considered and Decided Upon a Writ of Habeas Corpus, Allowed on the Petition of Charles Lockington, An Alien Enemy*. Philadelphia: Printed by John Binns.

Miller, Kerby. 1985. *Emigrants and Exiles: Ireland and the Irish Exodus to North America*. New York: Oxford University Press.

Scott, Kenneth, comp. 1979. *British Aliens in the United States during the War of 1812*. Baltimore: Genealogical Publishing.

Thomas, Isaiah, et al. 1874. *The History of Printing in America*. Worcester, MA: American Antiquarian Society.

Zagarri, Rosemarie. 2007. *Revolutionary Backlash: Women and Politics in the Early American Republic*. Philadelphia: University of Pennsylvania Press.

Zolberg, Aristide. 2006. *A Nation by Design: Immigration Policy in the Fashioning of America*. Cambridge, MA: Harvard University Press.

6

CIVILIZING THE WHITE MAN

· · · · · · · · · ·

American Indian Elites Define Citizenship in Oklahoma

KERRY WYNN

In the summer of 1926, Chickasaw citizen and Republican Party stalwart Estelle Chisholm Ward published the first issue of her new magazine, *The Super-Civilized Indian*. Filled with articles advocating political participation and advertisements for candidates, *The Super-Civilized Indian*, though short-lived, demonstrates an important and often-overlooked representation of American Indian citizenship. Ward's dedication to the magazine gestured to the ways in which some Oklahomans co-opted the language of civilization and portrayed the indigenous exercise of US citizenship as the responsibility of a more advanced and talented people. "To all North American Indians," Ward wrote,

> to my husband, a typical Chickasaw, to my son—an Amalgamating link between the "Man of Yesterday" and his "White Brother," an Oklahoman born and bred; to all Youth, whether of Red or White extraction—for you are fundamentally and intellectually the best boys and girls any generation or nation has ever known, is this magazine, "The Super-Civilized Indian" (Inc.) dedicated. (Ward 1926b, 1)

Providing a tribally specific location for herself through her husband and linking them both to the state of Oklahoma through their son, Ward looked forward to a new generation of American Indian and white Americans, who would govern together, given the explicitly political focus of the magazine.[1] Simultaneously encouraging pride in American Indian status and naturalizing white institutions, Ward used civilizationist discourse to assume a privileged position for some American Indian Oklahomans.

Ward's magazine and her use of the term "civilized" represent a particular moment in the development of the discourses on citizenship and civilization that had long haunted the exercise of political rights by American Indians in the United States. From the founding of the United States, American officials had insisted that civilization—most often defined exclusively as adherence to Euro-American cultural and social norms—was a prerequisite to the exercise of US citizenship for American Indians.[2] By the twentieth century, American Indian leaders had become adept at turning this discourse of civilization against US officials who sought to constrain American Indian behavior. As American Indian elites moved to consolidate their power in the new state of Oklahoma, they used the discourse of civilization, constructing an argument that American Indians were more civilized than Euro-Americans—in a sense, "super-civilized." This representation of American Indians accepted one premise of US Indian policy—that one must be "civilized" to be a citizen—but rejected the tandem premise that American Indians did not possess this civilization. On the contrary, Ward and others argued, many American Indians possessed a history and talents signifying advanced civilization and qualifying them not to learn but to exercise citizenship. Mounting a campaign to mobilize American Indian voters and to use history to assert American Indian cultural equality or superiority, Oklahoma American Indian elites sought to invigorate their power in Oklahoma and throughout the United States.

While contemporary scholars have produced valuable studies of the ways in which American Indians rejected or responded to American civilizationist discourse with the goal of demonstrating equality or protecting sovereignty, they have yet to critically address the manner in which certain American Indian authors deployed conceptions of civilization in order to suggest their superiority to white Americans.[3] The modern form of this subtlety of civilization discourse emerged in Indian Territory in the late 1800s and reached a new level in the state of Oklahoma in the 1920s.[4] Portrayals of "super-civilization" rested upon three key assertions that several authors sought to demonstrate: first, American Indians claimed a history on the North American continent that was more illustrious than Euro-Americans; second, contemporary American Indians excelled in modern, mainstream American society; and finally, American Indian leaders had not only a right but also a responsibility to participate in US politics because they were American Indian. Two magazines published in Oklahoma in the 1920s, *The Super-Civilized Indian* (published in 1926) and *The American Indian* (published from 1926 to 1930), used this particular civilization discourse to argue for an expanded role for American Indians as US citizens. Rather than turning away from their American Indian status, Estelle Chisholm Ward and Lee Harkins (Choctaw-Chickasaw editor of *The American Indian*) sought to place American Indians above Euro-Americans in a cultural and political hierarchy by recasting American Indian history and claiming state and national political rights.

In accepting civilizationist discourse but challenging its hierarchical underpinnings, advocates of super-civilization provided a potent argument for their own participation in the American polity but not for the protection of American Indian models of governance. Ward and Harkins assumed positions that distinguished American Indians from nonindigenous US citizens, not as a permanent underclass of American industrial democracy, but as leaders with distinctive assets to bring to the polity. Unlike previous generations of Indian Territory leaders, who used the discourse of civilization to defend tribal sovereignty, however, these editors articulated their claim to leadership in the American polity. Ward and Harkins did not advocate what many Native people wanted most—political autonomy—but sought rather mastery of US institutions.

This manifestation of discourse on civilization and citizenship owed its foundations to the specific context of Oklahoma's history and population. American Indian governments ruled the entire territory that would become Oklahoma until 1890; half of that territory would remain under the control of American Indian nations until statehood in 1907. The American Indian governments ruling the Indian Territory until 1907 were those of the "Five Civilized Tribes" (Cherokee, Choctaw, Chickasaw, Creek, and Seminole), who were given that title centuries before by European Americans because they adopted many trappings of European-derived cultures, such as Christianity, capitalism, and chattel slavery. Many American Indians in Oklahoma thus drew upon a long tradition of adaptation to Euro-American traditions, and they used this tradition to argue for greater rights or concessions from the American government. Throughout the nineteenth century, leaders of the nations of the Five Tribes pointed to their national institutions, such as boarding schools, court systems, and constitutional governments, in order to defend the sovereignty of these nations. In spite of these arguments, however, the American government forced the dissolution of the independent governments of the Five Tribes when Oklahoma became a state in 1907.

Citizens of the Five Tribes influenced American Indian politics in the 1920s, both as leaders of pan-Indian national organizations and as political pillars of the new state of Oklahoma. While these five nations represented only a handful of the dozens of nations represented in Oklahoma and the hundreds throughout the continental United States, they were numerically strong, with populations numbering into the tens of thousands. Their long histories of negotiation with the United States, early adoption of English-language education, and comparative wealth also positioned prominent citizens of the Five Tribes to navigate the worlds of state and national politics. The Five Tribes conceived of tribal membership as citizenship from the mid-nineteenth century, which imparted a facility with the terms and conditions of American political participation but enriched their understanding with a different context. Although the majority of citizens of the Five Tribes fought against their incorporation into the United States before the twentieth century, with Oklahoma's statehood, many channeled their activism into participation in the new state government.

The tenets of the discourse in "super-civilization" and citizenship owed a great deal to the position of power from which its adherents spoke, a direct result of their position as citizens of one of the Five Tribes and Oklahoma/US citizens. For generations, power and position in the territory derived from citizenship in and leadership of indigenous nations. Elite citizens of the Five Tribes assumed a privileged place in society. After statehood, with the entrenched family and political networks in the eastern half of the state, many Oklahoma politicians came from or courted those segments of the population. With the size of the Oklahoma American Indian population in general and their prominent connections, powerful Oklahoma American Indians could hope to influence state politics more than American Indians in most states. At Oklahoma's statehood day celebration in 1907, the new governor, Charles N. Haskell, demonstrated his willingness to court the subset of American Indian leaders who sought power in the new state government. Eliding the process of conquest that had preceded the formation of Oklahoma, Haskell delivered an inaugural address that focused on elevating American citizenship above all other forms of belonging and reached out to elites of the nations of the former Indian Territory:

> We are the first state where the original American, the owners of the soil, remained in large numbers as free and equal citizens with their white neighbors and took part in the formation and control of the state government. These nations that upon the laws of congress have the distinction of being named as the "Five Civilized Tribes" are united with their white neighbors on grounds of legal equality. Therefore the added pride in the flag of our country. We find the white stripe emblematic of the white race; we find the red emblematic of the red race, and uniting them beneath the field of azure blue we join heart and hand—the red and the white man—in saying Glory! Glory! Long live the State of Oklahoma.[5]

Although Haskell focused on uniting white and American Indian citizens of the new state, the institution of US government was a punishing turn for many indigenous Oklahomans. The allotment policy of the US government and the dissolution of sovereign American Indian governments preceding statehood reduced American Indian landholdings and removed government protection for cultural practices.[6] The process of statehood and ensuing political and economic developments left many American Indian communities divided along ideological, class, and racial lines. The recognition of the political power of elite American Indians in Oklahoma by figures such as Haskell, combined with the awareness of discrimination against American Indians both in Oklahoma and outside of the state, created the conditions for a new order of claims to cultural, social, and political position.

In using the discourse of civilization, Estelle Ward and Lee Harkins accessed terms formative to the character of federal Indian programs. Throughout the early twentieth century, American politicians and administrators kept civilization at the forefront of federal discussions of American Indian policy. The Dawes Act of 1887, which organized American Indian citizenship in the United States until 1924, extended US citizenship to allottees and American Indians "who [had] adopted the habits of civilized life."[7] Even the Meriam Report of 1928, commonly credited with revealing the abuses of federal policy and ushering in a new era in Indian affairs, relied upon conceptions of civilization, associating the term with "white" or "dominant" and judging programs on their ability to impart an understanding of civilization to American Indians (Institute for Government Research 1928). Perhaps most importantly, although the Indian Citizenship Act of 1924, which granted American citizenship to those American Indians who did not yet possess it, contained no mention of civilization, there were clear reminders from other states, where the demonstration of "civilization"—sometimes necessitating the renunciation of tribal affiliation—was required for voting eligibility, that state legislatures and courts clearly endangered American Indian political rights throughout the United States (McCool 1992).[8]

With the publication of their respective magazines, Estelle Chisholm Ward and Lee Harkins presented a counterpoint to the federal perspective on American Indian political participation. These two publications, *The Super-Civilized Indian* and *The American Indian*, provide examples of the rhetorical and ideological moves many Oklahoma American Indian elites made in order to represent American Indian citizenship in terms that debunked old stereotypes. They also indicate the consequences of continuing to use the term *civilization* in order to characterize a laudable form of political belonging. Turning the discourse of civilization back on US politicians and writers was a subversive move in the context of American national culture. However, it was also something that would be assumed by elite citizens of the Choctaw and Chickasaw nations from whence these editors came. Lee Harkins was the descendant of a prominent Choctaw political family, and Estelle Chisholm Ward, who also traced her ancestors to famous Indian Territory residents, attended and later taught at the flagship Chickasaw school for women (Wright 1959, 286; Thoburn and Wright 1929, 748).

The political context of the era rendered the interrogation of "civilization" relevant—perhaps even necessary—to the demand for American Indian citizenship rights, but the manner in which these Oklahomans adopted a discourse of superior civilization was not accepted by all American Indians. Many American Indians rejected participation in the American political system—instead insisting on the exclusive sovereignty of American Indian nations—and protested their very inclusion in the American polity, which had been accomplished without their consent. In addition, American Indians who used the discourse of civilization to assert their power at times professed elitist and racist ideas, alienating American Indians with African ancestry and American Indians who criticized elites for amassing wealth at the expense of their fellow tribal members.[9] The discourse of "super-civilization" was not necessarily a pluralistic discourse. *The American Indian* accepted or encouraged associations with whiteness, highlighted what they termed "progressive" activities, and at the very least failed to disrupt the use of civilizationist discourse to oppress black Americans.

The first claim to advanced civilization by these American Indian elites rested on a reconstruction of American Indian history. For Harkins and Ward, it was their American Indian ancestry that qualified them to claim superiority, distinguishing them from the undelineated masses. As a contributor to *The American Indian* insisted, "The Indian who becomes a white man and forgets his ancestors is as colorless and uninteresting as the millions of other standardized materialists whose ranks he has joined."[10] *The American Indian* provided histories of specific tribes and individuals intended to convey the role of American Indians in the development of the United States, the abuse of American Indians by Europeans and their descendants, and political and scientific achievements of American Indian societies. The tribally specific nature of these articles is essential, given the focus of early historians on the homogenizing aspects of pan-Indian movements of the 1920s and 1930s (see Hertzberg 1971). Rather than portraying American Indians as a single entity, these stories related distinctive histories of widely varying nations with claims to civilization often surpassing those of Europeans. Many articles focused on nations among the Five Tribes, such as the Creeks, but others recounted historical facts about other nations, such as Osages or Shawnees, and individuals including Pushmataha, Tecumseh, and Sequoyah, among others (Lindsey 1926a, 1926b; Holden 1927; Carter 1926; Davis 1927). Communication scholar John M. Coward has characterized the history constructed in *The American Indian* as "idealistic" and supportive of a "'great man' approach to the past," with the effect of supporting contemporary paternalism, but these characteristics also communicated to non-Native audiences the reordering of civilizationist hierarchies (Coward 1997, 11).

While many articles in the pages of *The American Indian* detailed military conflict, most authors were careful to note cooperation between American Indians and European colonists and US citizens and emphasized that later American Indian battles against these groups were defensive struggles to maintain their land base (Madden 1928b; Parker 1928).[11] These articles served as corrective responses to contemporary narratives of history and pointed to examples of American Indian allies of Europeans and their descendants, such as the Oneidas, "who many times helped and protected the Colonists, although they were attacked by both British and Indian forces for doing this."[12] Emphasis on American Indian subsistence and military support of British colonists and the United States figured prominently in these tales of American political development, which credited American Indians with saving the American nation. *The Super-Civilized Indian* carried the theme of historic cooperation between American Indians and the United States on its cover, in the form of an illustration of an American Indian in buckskin and headdress handing a pipe to Uncle Sam. The American Indian cover figure, dressed in the attire of Plains tribes and depicted in front of tipis, speaks more to the traditions of American Indians outside of the Five Tribes and indicates the tendency of publishers to use Plains peoples as symbolic representations of all American Indians.

Authors included in *The American Indian* also used history to contradict the stereotype of American Indians as bloodthirsty and vicious. These authors elaborated on the abuses suffered by American Indians at the hands of white Americans and focused on forced removal of American Indians by the federal government, the usurpation of American Indian land through government and individual action, and the breaking of treaties by the United States (Flagg 1927; LaMere 1927; Madden 1928a; Hammond 1928; Jones 1927).[13] These articles were important to asserting American Indian civilization because charges that the American Indian was a "cruel and merciless savage" in the past formed a significant portion of the anti-Indian discourse of the early twentieth century.[14] Harkins called attention to hypocrisy and inaccuracy in the writing of white journalists and historians:

Giving such a title as being a "Famous Indian Fighter" to the casual reader perhaps conveys very little meaning. To a person of Indian blood he sees "no glory" in such an uttered vocative for the departed warrior. . . . Because many of the Indians fought before they yielded their warm firesides and homes and to leave the graves of their forefathers . . . the whiteman is eulogized by his race for having been an Indian fighter. Since the Indian never refers to his forefather as a "Famous Whiteman Fighter" then why can't we expect such an ethical observance from the white writer![15]

The alternate vision of history the articles in *The American Indian* proffered sought to turn the American narrative of defense against American Indian aggression on its head by pointing to the glory given to "Indian Fighters" and US aggression against American Indian communities. These articles shamed white Americans for failing to realize the abuses against American Indians by their ancestors and disputed the claims of whites to civilization not only for these violent acts but also for the way they were memorialized in contemporary society. Europeans and Euro-Americans were the "savages," not American Indians, these authors argued.[16]

The histories written by contributors to *The American Indian* also provided evidence of past American Indian achievements, asserting the existence of American Indian civilization in previous eras and delineating American Indian contributions to contemporary politics and society. These narratives of past achievements served as an important counterpoint to Americans who insisted that American Indians had not yet reached a stage of advanced civilization. Indeed, they demonstrated the importance of American Indians to constructing US society by imparting advances in civilization to less advanced Euro-Americans. Some of these articles credited American Indians with the founding of Oklahoma society. The first issue of the magazine, in fact, critiqued historical portrayals of Oklahoma that ignored the important role of Indian Territory as its foundations. Harkins, the editor of the magazine, found it "irksome to an Indian's soul for some of the state's budding editorialists to say that Oklahoma was a 'wild and wooley' place before statehood" (Harkins 1926a). Harkins soon moved on to include articles crediting American Indians with creating the structure of government adopted by the United States and detailing the scientific advances Mayans made (Madden 1928c; Hobart 1930; Henry 1930).[17]

The portrayal of historic American Indian societies provided a foundation from which to argue for the superiority of American Indian cultures to Euro-American cultures. Harkins indicated the implication of articles regarding American Indian inventions:

It gets rather disgusting to a reader when an author refers to the Indian as a "savage or barbarian" as if he never had a real cultural background. The Indian did not just "happen" but must have gone through as many stages in man development as his white brother. . . . It is a known fact that about the time that Babylon was such a seat of learning that the Mayan progress in Yucatan was at its height and perhaps as venerable. . . . The Indian can point with pride to his cultural background, ever remembering that he represents the oldest aristocracy in this so called new world. The name "barbarian" is a misnomer applied to him by any Anglo-Saxon writer, whose folk at one time were clothing themselves in skins and sleeping in drifted leaves of the forest. (Harkins 1930)

Reference to American Indians as members of the "oldest aristocracy" was an integral part of Harkins's positioning of American Indians and the ideological work he hoped to accomplish with his magazine (Harkins 1926b). The history of the continent was the history of American Indians, who had distinguished themselves through an illustrious history that surpassed the history of Europeans in its developments.

The publishers of Oklahoma American Indian magazines in the 1920s also aimed to establish the importance of American Indians as contributors to contemporary American institutions. *The Super-Civilized Indian* prominently featured American Indian Oklahomans who participated in voluntary and political organizations and showcased materials from these organizations.[18] In the pages of *The American Indian*, Lee Harkins referred to American Indians as "a potent part of today's society" and published articles that portrayed American Indian groups as "a class among those who constitute the backbone of good citizens," who "gave more and sacrificed more in proportion to their numbers than any other class of people in the United States during [World War I]" (Fenwick 1926).[19] In addition to educating audiences about the superior achievements of American Indians, so that "all people" might "know Indians as Indians know each other," Estelle Ward criticized contemporary ways of describing American Indians that devalued their contributions to the United States (Ward 1926c). She argued vehemently against the use of "Poor Lo," to refer to American Indians, for "Though an Indian were *starving* in the *gutter*, to *himself* and to us, he would *never* be 'Poor Lo,' but, proud, in his poverty and degradation [*sic*] to *know*, that he is an *American Indian*. And *rich* in the knowledge of what *that* means today" (Ward 1926d). American Indian history was a source of pride, and the vote was to be a source of power. Ward included figures of the American Indian population of Oklahoma at statehood under the title "All Are Now Voters" in order to emphasize the strength of American Indian interests in the state and demonstrate the advantage to politicians in gaining the American Indian vote (Ward 1926a). The number of advertisements for political candidates in the pages of *The Super-Civilized Indian* shows that many took American Indian voting interests seriously.[20]

Of course, *The American Indian* and *The Super-Civilized Indian* did not exist in a vacuum, and each magazine showed the influence of mainstream American culture in the 1920s. In this era, government officials, magazine writers, and politicians not only questioned the civilization of American Indians but also the civilization of all non-Anglo cultures. Although cultural relativism had gained a foothold in some circles, many Anglo-Americans cast groups such as southern and eastern Europeans, Africans, and Asians (as well as American Indians) as uncivilized. Rather than question the basis for the suspicions cast upon all groups believed to be lacking civilization, Oklahoma American Indian elites co-opted the terminology used by Anglo nativist groups. In *The American Indian*, authors labeled American Indians "the original 100 per cent Americans," adopting a US slogan often used during World War I and the 1920s to encourage patriotism and block immigration, a phrase that conjured suspicion of immigrants who were portrayed by nativists as uncivilized and undesirable.[21] Authors also claimed for American Indians the role of "true American[s]" and "original Americans" (Smith 1926). This redefinition or historicizing of the term "American" pointed to the role American Indian elites expected to exercise in the United States and indicted attempts to deny American citizenship rights to American Indians. However, it also played into the stereotypes of other ethnic groups, merely adding Anglo-Americans to the mix.

Given the portrayal of the enviable history and desirable qualities of American Indians, editors and authors urged American Indians to become involved in the American political system, portraying political and social participation as a responsibility of American Indian men and women. *The Super-Civilized Indian* was, at its core, a magazine that encouraged American Indian political participation and involvement in partisan politics. Estelle Ward acknowledged to the readers of her magazine its role as a vehicle for political candidates to reach voters, but emphasized that taking action should be the audience's priority:

> We recommend for your earnest consideration these candidates who are advertising with us, and ask that you look well, into what their

lives *have been* and *are* as private citizens; and weigh, unbiased, the things they are promising you as officials—*Then vote*. (Ward 1926e)

Both Democrats and Republicans recorded appeals to American Indian voters in the pages of *The Super-Civilized Indian*. These appeals validated American Indian political participation, as in the case of the Democratic Party, which recognized the "high official places" held by American Indians and the "splendid services rendered by them." The Democratic Party also played upon patriotism and the "100 per cent Americanism" noted above: "The Indian citizen is really the true American. The Democratic party is really the American party" (Key 1926). Advertisers in *The Super-Civilized Indian* distinguished themselves as candidates through their identities as American Indians or their interest in American Indian concerns.

Authors in the pages of these magazines joined the possession of a superior degree of civilization to a mission to use that civilization to improve the United States. Arthur C. Parker, in a letter to *The American Indian*, proposed that "all Americans of Indian ancestry [have] a double responsibility to do a bit more than Americans who have not the blood of the old stock—and this in spite of every handicap" (Parker 1926). The agenda of the Tushkahoma League, published in *The Super-Civilized Indian*, included the following admonition:

We hereby further urge upon every member of the Indian Tribes the imperative necessity and importance of exercising their elective franchise. It is our weapon of defense. We are not good citizens if we fail to do our patriotic duty of voting. (Tushkahoma League 1927)

The duty of voting was but one specific aspect of the call by American Indian elites for American Indians to seek leadership positions. Lee Harkins suggested in 1928 that "it is about time that an Aboriginal is due to sit in the most honored chair in the United States," lobbying for an American Indian "president of the U.S. in the near future" (Harkins 1928). With their depiction of young adults and youths who were promised to be the future of the state and the nation, these magazines envisioned a new generation of American Indian leaders for the 1920s and beyond.

In their discussion of the sense of mission American Indians should possess and the degree of power they might someday hold, adherents to the idea of superior civilization of American Indians could prove quite empowering for American Indian citizens of the United States. However, the adoption of the ideology of civilization in this manner had definite limitations. By continuing to use terms European Americans imposed in early generations to constrain American Indian behavior, magazines such as these kept the terms alive and validated a limited range of behaviors. They expanded "civilization" to include American Indian cultures, but they did not mount a defense of American Indian sovereignty, assuming instead that the result of the recognition of civilization was participation in the United States. Those who participated in this discourse accepted that they had become citizens of the United States and that was where their fortunes were to be found. Note that the articles referenced above reified American Indian history, not contemporary American Indian separatist movements.

This wholehearted adoption of American citizenship, when combined with the focus on "progressiveness" and the alliance with white Americans these magazines portrayed, indicated the painful and detrimental omissions of these images of superior civilization. The constant comparison to white Americans contributors employed indicated that they had accepted the racialist discourse that encouraged white supremacy over African Americans. For the most part, the editors ignored the history of slavery of the Five Tribes and the struggles of contemporary Afro-Indian people to be heard within indigenous nations or the United States. The omission of African Americans, more numerous in the state than American Indians, was in many cases conspicuous, as in the constant repetition of "white" and "red" paired with each other. While fighting for the rights of American Indians, these magazines ignored the Jim Crow segregation African Americans faced daily in Oklahoma and throughout the nation and the legacies of slavery within indigenous nations. On the rare occasions writers mentioned African Americans, it was generally to deny that American Indians had anything to do with them, as the reader who considered it an "insult" to suggest that Chickasaws, Cherokees, and Choctaws had "intermingled with the negro" (S. L. C. 1931). Statements such as these denied the existence and rights of citizens with African and American Indian ancestors within the Five Tribes. A more critical view of the term *civilization* surely would not eliminate racism among Oklahoma American Indian elites; it was too ideologically entrenched among them. Perhaps, however, the refusal to represent citizenship in terms of civilization could have opened a space to eviscerate the racial hierarchy whites had constructed, instead of rearranging the order of its categories.

Although they fell short of revolutionary, the pages of *The Super-Civilized Indian* and *The American Indian* reveal an intricate and vigorous portrayal of the connection between civilization and citizenship for American Indians. Rather than accepting the US portrayal of American Indian lack of civilization as a rationale for their disenfranchisement, some American Indian elites in Oklahoma argued that American Indians' claim to a superior form of civilization fitted them for and demanded active participation in citizenship roles. As an article reprinted in *The American Indian* prophesied,

> Savagery, brutality, barbarism, civilization, education and reason are but ways of thinking. . . . That the Red race through its best representatives will live and become active forces in civilization is demonstrated by the very eloquence and logic of the leaders of that race. (Parker 1916)

This excerpt summarized the views of many Oklahoma American Indian elites who addressed civilizationist discourse in the 1920s and went on to be national leaders of American Indian movements in the 1930s. Casting American Indian citizenship rights in this manner certainly had disadvantages, as it could not fundamentally unsettle or divorce the concepts of civilization and citizenship from each other, and actually may have limited the development of a more pluralistic discourse that might present greater possibilities to a more diverse array of American Indians. The assertion of superior civilization presented opportunities for the elites who crafted the discourse, however, who emphasized the importance of American Indian history and contemporary American Indian participation in the American polity, implying by their works that they were capable of and committed to civilizing the white man.

NOTES

1. Ward's dedication to her husband and son indicates the influence of gendered expectations for social and political participation. Ward's daughter would be featured in a later issue of the magazine, and Ward herself was an enrolled member of the Chickasaw nation with prominent Cherokee ancestors. Although this would have been known by many of the readers in the relatively small population of Oklahoma, she chose to draw a masculine link between American Indians and white Americans.

2. For example, the Treaty of Holston (between the United States and the Cherokee Nation) promised monetary aid to Cherokees so they may be "led to a higher degree of civilization." The idea behind this "civilization program," pursued most prominently in the administrations of Washington and Jefferson, was to gradually incorporate American Indians into the United States. "Treaty with the Cherokee, 1791," July 2, 1791. | 7 Stat., 39. | Proclamation, Feb. 7, 1792, in Kappler (1904, 31).

3. Although the literature on this specific use of civilizationist discourse to build a position of Native superiority is slight, Amy Ware's *The Cherokee Kid* indicates its development, and there is a sophisticated body of work on American Indian facility with and adaptation of Euro-American ideals. John M. Coward has written about *The American Indian*'s promotion of an assimilationist progressive movement, but this article proposes that considering what Coward describes as Lee Harkins's idealistic construction of history and urge for assimilation as an argument for superior qualification gives greater insight into discourses on citizenship (Coward 1997). For works that address American Indian uses of and opposition to concepts of "civilization," see Bess (2000); Hertzberg (1971); Maddox (2005); and Ware (2015).

4. I have argued elsewhere that during the late nineteenth century, Cherokees and other members of the "Five Civilized Tribes" used an early manifestation of the discourse of social superiority employed in the 1920s. See Wynn (2009).

5. "Transcript of Statehood Proceedings." *NewsOK*, http://newsok.com/article/3169808?mp=1&pg=3.

6. For details on the devastating effects of the allotment of the lands that became the eastern half of Oklahoma for their American Indian owners, see Debo ([1940] 1984).

7. An Act to Provide for the Allotment of Lands in Severalty to Indians on the Various Reservations (General Allotment Act or Dawes Act), Statutes at Large 24, 388–91, Native American Documents Project Document A1887.

8. Oklahomans were aware of discrimination in other states. See "Special Act of Congress on March 3, 1901, Granted Citizenship to Five Tribe Members," *The American Indian* 1 (10) (1927): 7.

9. For example, see "Carlisle Not a Mixed School," *The American Indian* 1 (6) (1927): 8.

10. "Wanted—Enlightened Indians," *The American Indian* 1 (1) (1926): 12.

11. See also "Indians Loyal to Uncle Sam," *The American Indian* 1 (2) (1926): 12. "Famous Indian Fighter' Dies," *The American Indian* 1 (4) (1926): 8. "Indians'

Culinary Art Greatly Aided American Colonists," *The American Indian* 1 (10) (1927): 13. "There Are Many Facts History Books Do Not Tell," *The American Indian* 2 (9) (1928): 14.

12. Untitled article. *The American Indian* 3 (3) (1928): 4.

13. See also "Taxing Indian Land," *The American Indian* 2 (9) (1928): 4.

14. "Telling the Truth," *The American Indian* 2 (10) (1928): 4.

15. "Famous 'Indian Fighter' Dies," *The American Indian* 1 (3) (1926): 8.

16. "Our Government Patterned after Iroquois Confederacy," *The American Indian* 1 (12) (1927): 8.

17. See also "Racial Achievements," *The American Indian* 1 (12) (1927): 4.

18. "Mrs. Czarina Colbert Conlan," *The Super-Civilized Indian* 1 (1) (1926): 5. "Hon. William A. Durant," *The Super-Civilized Indian* 1 (2) (1926): 4. "William Thomas Ward," *The Super-Civilized Indian* 1 (3) (1926): 8. "The Choctaw-Chickasaw Protective Association," *The Super-Civilized Indian* 1 (1) (1926): 3. "Tishomingo Daughters," *The Super-Civilized Indian* 1 (3) (1926): 4.

19. See also "Background and History of Oklahoma Is Typical Indian," *The American Indian* 1 (1) (1926): 3. "Miss Rogers, Osage Indian Princes, Talks over Radio at Philadelphia," *The American Indian* 1 (3) (1926): 2.

20. The first issue contained five pages of political advertisements. *The Super-Civilized Indian* 1 (1) (1926).

21. "A New Publication," *The American Indian* 1 (2) (1926): 8. "Real American History," *The American Indian* 2 (2) (1927): 4.

WORKS CITED

Bess, Jennifer. 2000. "'Kill the Indian and Save the Man!': Charles Eastman Surveys His Past." *Wicazo Sa Review* 15 (1): 7–28.

Carter, Chas. D. 1926. "Memorable Debate between Pushmataha and Tecumseh." *The American Indian* 1 (1): 14–15.

Coward, John M. 1997. "Promoting the Progressive Indian: Lee Harkins and *The American Indian Magazine.*" *American Journalism* 14 (1): 3–18.

Davis, James A. 1927. "Sequoyah Is Called 'Intellectual Genius' of the New World." *The American Indian* 1 (4): 14–15.

Debo, Angie. [1940] 1984. *And Still the Waters Run: The Betrayal of the Five Civilized Tribes.* Norman: University of Oklahoma Press.

Fenwick, C. S. 1926. "The Rural Cherokees Are Very Devout Christians." *The American Indian* 1 (2): 16.

Flagg, Sybil. 1927. "Ohioan Tells of Ruthlessness against the American Indian." *The American Indian* 1 (12): 7.

Hammond, Hala Jean. 1928. "Indians Voiced Resentment for Opening Up of Their Land." *The American Indian* 2 (8): 6.

Harkins, Lee. 1926a. "Background and History of Oklahoma Is Typical Indian." *The American Indian* 1 (1): 3.

———. 1926b. "Dedication." *The American Indian* 1 (1): 1.

———. 1928. "Presidential Possibilities." *The American Indian* 2 (6): 4.

———. 1930. "Culture of the Indian." *The American Indian* 4 (4): 4.

Henry, Thomas R. 1930. "Constitution Idea from Indians." *The American Indian* 4 (11): 7.

Hertzberg, Hazel. 1971. *The Search for American Indian Identity: Modern Pan-Indian Movements*. Syracuse: Syracuse University Press.

Hobart, Harry K. 1930. "Ancient Mayan Mathematicians Ones Who Invented Zero." *The American Indian* 4 (10): 8.

Holden, Geneva E. 1927. "'Last Supper Ceremony' Observed by Shawnees for Departed Ones." *The American Indian* 1 (7): 9.

Institute for Government Research. 1928. *The Problem of Indian Administration*. Baltimore: Johns Hopkins Press, 1928.

Jones, Dr. Howard. 1927. "French and English Played Santa Role in Gaining of Ohio." *The American Indian* 2 (1): 5.

Kappler, Charles J., ed. 1904. *Indian Affairs: Laws and Treaties*. Vol. 2, *Treaties* (Washington, DC: Government Printing Office, 1904).

Key, Geo. D. 1926. "Why Our Oklahoma Indian Should Vote the Democratic Ticket." *The Super-Civilized Indian* 1 (1): 8.

LaMere, Oliver. 1927. "The Tragic Removal of the Winnebagoes to Nebraska." *The American Indian* 1 (11): 7.

Lindsey, Lilah D. 1926a. "Claremore Named after Slain Osage Chief in 1828." *The American Indian* 1 (2): 7.

———. 1926b. "'Green Corn Dance' of the Creeks Lasted for Three Days and Nights." *The American Indian* 1 (2): 5.

Madden, John. 1928a. "Choctaws, First as Body, to Traverse 'Trail of Tears.'" *The American Indian* 2 (7): 3.

———. 1928b. "Pawnee Scouts Aided in Annexation of Sunny California." *The American Indian* 2 (5): 6.

———. 1928c. "Were the Maya Race Descendants of the 'Lost Atlantis'?" *The American Indian* 2 (4): 3.

Maddox, Lucy. 2005. *Citizen Indians: Native American Intellectuals, Race, and Reform*. Ithaca, NY: Cornell University Press.

McCool, Daniel. 1992. "Indian Voting." In *American Indian Policy in the Twentieth Century*, edited by Vine Deloria, 105–15. Norman: University of Oklahoma Press.

Parker, Arthur C. 1916. "The Editor's Viewpoint: The Civilizing Power of Language." *Quarterly Journal of the Society of American Indians* 4 (2): 128.

———. 1926. Letter to the Editor. *The American Indian* 1 (2): 8.

———. 1928. "Fourth Friday in September Is to Be Known as Indian Day." *The American Indian* 2 (8): 2.

S. L. C. 1931. "Criticism of 'Cimarron.'" *The American Indian* 5 (4): 4.

Smith, Juanita Johnston. 1926. "The Maid That Was Made in America." *The Super-Civilized Indian* 1 (2): 8.

Thoburn, Joseph, and Muriel H. Wright. 1929. "Estelle Chisholm Ward." In *Oklahoma: A History of the State and Its People*. Vol. 4. New York: Lewis Historical Publishing.

Tushkahoma League. 1927. "Indians of Oklahoma Organized to Exercise Power of Vote." *The American Indian* 2 (1): 6.

Ward, Estelle Chisholm. 1926a. "All Are Now Voters." *The Super-Civilized Indian* 1 (3): 8–9.

———. 1926b. "Dedication." *The Super-Civilized Indian* 1 (1): 1.

———. 1926c. "Editorial." *The Super-Civilized Indian* 1 (1): 6.

———. 1926d. "'Poor Lo' and 'The Squaw Man.'" *The Super-Civilized Indian* 1 (1): 10. Emphasis in original.

———. 1926e. "To Our Readers." *The Super-Civilized Indian* 1 (1): 7. Emphasis in original.

Ware, Amy. 2015. *The Cherokee Kid: Will Rogers, Tribal Identity, and the Making of an American Icon*. Lawrence: University Press of Kansas.

Wright, Muriel H. 1959. "Lee F. Harkins, Choctaw." *Chronicles of Oklahoma* 37: 285–87.

Wynn, Kerry. 2009. "'Miss Indian Territory and Mr. Oklahoma Territory': Marriage, Settlement, and Citizenship in the Indian Territory and the United States." In *Moving Subjects: Gender, Mobility, and Intimacy in an Age of Global Empire*, edited by Tony Ballantyne and Antoinette Burton, 172–89. Urbana: University of Illinois Press.

7

MUSEUM-MAKING

· · · · · · · · · ·

"New" Canadians Reimagine Heritage and Citizenship

SUSAN L. T. ASHLEY

This chapter explores how heritage institutions, particularly museums, contribute to practices of democracy as spaces and media of knowledge-building used by "new" Canadians. What is represented in a museum, a public space, can affect how Canadian society sees itself, how outsiders see us, and who is defined as belonging to this community as citizens. Museums have historically been situated at the intersection of representation and citizenship, as both formally and informally inscribed. They represent and authenticate official statements about meaning and belonging, while at the same time serving as "neutral" public spaces for knowledge-building and citizen participation. Museums legitimize versions of a state or community's history, what is accepted as heritage, who belongs to that heritage, who has membership and status within a community, and who does not belong. And expressions of nondominant players may be included or appropriated by this institution. Yet at the same time they serve as informal public spaces or arenas for social interaction and dialogue. The balancing of these seemingly incommensurate roles has been a central question in museology—representing and shaping citizens on one hand, and on the other serving as site and tool for alternative meaning-making, expressions, and participation in culture, heritage, and citizenship.

The study and representation of culture and heritage—of the significance, meaning, and value of various expressions and products—has traditionally been a domain of museums. Object collecting, conservation, research,
exhibition, and education have been typically the institution's historic role,
a role set within the context of nation-state and colonialism. But contemporary museums are under considerable pressure to address the relationship
between identity and citizenship in response to social, cultural, and economic
processes of nation-building and globalization. Increasingly they are called
on to represent cultural difference as well as homogeneity. The troubled history of museums as re-presenters of dominant cultural perspectives has been
explored throughout the literature. Described as "central tools of modernity"
(Bennett 2006, 56), current literature recognizes that museums do not act
simply as a "neutral, sheltering places for objects" (Duncan 1995, 10), but,
more likely, they "generate ideological effects for constructing and com-
municating a particular vision of society" (Sandell 2007, 3). Museums have
been situated as an apparatus of the nation-state, constructing and com-
municating nation-state identity and applying Foucauldian social control,
but also as an important site in the bourgeois public sphere (Bennett 1995;
Macdonald 2003). As well, there is large body of literature delving into the
colonial tendencies of museums and their troubling relationships to "Others"
(Boast 2011). This discourse about the role and public nature of museums
questions the very business of representation and advocates a decentering of
the museum toward a nonauthoritative position.

While most of these practices of knowledge-building and representation
occur within and in relation to traditional museums, my research inspected
the museological practices that take place beyond these institutions in the
informal actions of communities. The word *community* is invoked here in a
flexible sense: as groups of people who come together in some kind of formation that is public. Through various media forms, community members pub-
licize, or "make public," their visions of self and community outside of formal
institutions. The term *new Canadians* is also a phrase that is used conditionally
in this chapter, itself an imaginary designating non-English or non-French
residents (Smith 2014). What happens to people's sense of heritage when
their lives are disrupted or marginalized and they have moved as immigrants
away from their country of origin? How do migrating people decide the
things they want to keep and pass on to future generations? How do migrant
peoples rearticulate and represent their heritage through museum-making

practices? And further, how is this used as a means to assert citizenship in their new countries? Of particular interest are the ways that immigrants use museological practices in this struggle to self-represent—and in Canada this includes a range of institutions such as the Sikh Gurdwara museum and the Nikkei community center in British Columbia, the Ukrainian Heritage Village in Alberta, and the Black Cultural Centre in Nova Scotia. This chapter explores how museum-making by two immigrant groups in Canada invokes imaginaries of heritage and practices of citizenship. I look at the ways that heritage is being used by uprooted people as a signifier of desired membership in their new locations and as a signifier of resistance. I consider whether or not *new* articulations of heritage, new public formations, and new ideas about citizenship are created through these practices.

MUSEUMS AND SOCIAL IMAGINARIES

The kinds of knowledge that are represented or "made public" in museums about community and citizen membership involves a particular vision, a social imaginary in the words of Charles Taylor (2002), or an imagined community, according to Benedict Anderson (1983). A social imaginary enables the systems and practices of a society by narrating a sense of it—it is a shared idea about the nature of a community perpetuated through communal discourse. Representation through social institutions is key to the imaginary's perpetuation, but like representation, these are "imaginary," that is, works of creation and communication.

The representation of social imaginaries expressed through museum practices can occur on two levels: in formal institutions and in the informal actions of members of the community (Ashley 2005). We are most familiar with formal museum institutions—public buildings, often of monumental architectural scale, with halls exhibiting materials from the natural or cultural history. They hold symbolic power in our society, acting as important places for the accumulation of information, communication, material, and financial resources, and shaping the ways in which information and symbolic content are produced and circulated in society (Thompson 1995). Innis (1951) discusses such institutions as holding a "monopoly of knowledge," a centralized structure of power, situated in an imposing city building, controlling the preservation of historical knowledge and identity of the dominant culture, and also world knowledge seen through the lens of the dominant culture. In Canada, such museums have taken steps to incorporate diverse cultural experiences in their exhibitions, usually in the context of settlement and immigration narratives (Gordon-Walker 2013).

At the informal level, museum institutions have also historically acted as spaces in the public sphere for social gathering and exchange. This has been explored as a means of social control where "making appearances" in public spaces ensured that persons knew their place in social hierarchies (Bourdieu 1984), but also more recently as community "contact zones" that accommodate meaning-making and dialogue among publics (Clifford 1997). That visitors bring their own interpretations to representations made in museum exhibits is accepted in the museum literature (Hooper-Greenhill 1992) and is an indication of how the museum space fosters independent knowledge-making on the part of the public.

HERITAGE AND CITIZENSHIP

The concepts of "Heritage" and "Citizenship" are parts of this social imaginary, which underpin personal and collective identities. Both concepts are used as identity indictors of membership in states (political entities with geographic boundaries) and in nations ("whole way of life" cultural or ethnic group formations). Heritage encompasses the foundational assemblage of traditions, ideas, and things from the past that a nation or a state wants to pass on to future generations (Hall 2000). Citizenship is typically used as a marker of someone's status within a state and to describe the formalized practices related to certain rights and duties within that state (Isin and Wood 1999). Both heritage and citizenship are invoked in disputes over membership in these community formations, identifying who belongs and who does not. So the potential politics of both words is important, and public statements and in-public positioning made in places like museums wield significant power. The historic role of national museums, for example, has been to construct and make public official statements about heritage, thus giving an official stamp of legitimacy to particular versions of heritage, but also to legitimize particular versions of citizenship.

Heritage is an imaginary, in relation to the past, used by people to give meaning to their identity on individual and community scales—a complex of values, symbols, meanings, and relationships that, importantly, is an affective process. It appeals to an emotional or affective sense of historical cultural legacy that contributes to present-day identity and a sense of communally shared signification of aspects of the past, but it also represents a blatant desire to colonize the future with those meanings (Ashworth 2008). Heritage is used on individual and on communal scales, and is framed as process and as "things." The emotional and imaginative use of heritage can be seen as a conscious and an unconscious process. Heritage can be understood as a particular historical construct we intentionally build but also as the unarticulated background or part of the "cultural baggage" we carry around with us. Not a "thing" that "is," but an unconscious environment or a background noise that is normalized in the present, and, a building block in the development of personal identity. It is possible to think of heritage as one part of Bennett's "logic of culture," the process of working on and transforming the self that arises from the ongoing tension between the unconscious traditions we inherit and the self-conscious efforts we make throughout our lives to strive for individuality (Bennett 2006, 52). Deciding what parts of these unconscious traditions to keep and pass on between generations becomes an emotional decision about choices.

On a collective level, self-conscious efforts to construct identity might embrace and project a particular version of heritage or tradition. Here the potential politics of heritage becomes important, where public represen- tations about heritage, such as those in museum exhibits, have particular meanings. So heritage in its collective form is then about power. Smith (2006) argues that heritage is a cultural and political practice that does work in the present, especially to socially legitimize or to exclude individuals and cultures. It is a reflection of power structures, an instrument in the exercise of power, and, as Ashworth (2008) points out, a colonization by power struc- tures into the future. So choices, political choices, are made as to what is included and excluded in the communal articulation of heritage—including membership or citizenship status.

This is where museums and other institutions of heritage, as re-presenters and communicators of versions of heritage, come into play—where social imaginaries are given their official stamp of legitimacy. Museum display is a public act, a performance about social identity, and its public-ness makes it consequential. And the use of museums by nation-states to make public, official statements about heritage, and to represent particular versions of citi- zenship, has been well explored in the museum literature (Allen and Anson 2005; Macdonald 2003; Peach 2005). Some argue that not only were museums historically used to define and assert cohesive national identities, but they con- tinue to be employed to achieve such goals through "social inclusion" policies (Message 2009).

Both "heritage" and "citizenship" continue to be linked to *place*, particularly to bounded nation-states. Ashworth, Graham, and Tunbridge (2007) write that heritage is often misinterpreted to be locations that possess inherent qualities, a "sense of place" that bestows identity. Official designation of places as "heritage" can be seen as a signification of place by which a state declares ownership of a particular location—a symbolic territorial claim. But Ashworth, Graham, and Tunbridge argue that much social and political identification has no particular need to be rooted in a particular place. Identity, community, and heritage are capable of being "de-rooted and re-rooted" as people reconfigure their relationship to time and space.

Thus I am interested in how this imaginary called heritage, used by people to define a collective identity and also citizen membership, changes when "place" can no longer be assumed as an identity marker. When people have moved as immigrants to a new location far away from their country of origin, they are removed from both political places and places to which they may have attached heritage significance. How do they redefine their identities, their place in community, their senses of heritage? And while this constitutes part of my broader research interest, I offer here ideas and empirical work I have done among ethnic minorities in Canada, both new immigrants and those born in Canada, to contribute to broader discussions about identity, heritage, citizenship, and museums. I explore in this chapter two museum-related projects undertaken by minority groups in Canada who are perceived by white Canadians as not "real" Canadians. I am interested in the motivations behind the undertaking of these projects, how these people express the projects' relationship to their "heritage," how the museum projects are used as a medium of communication to transmit ideas and values, and in what ways these projects articulate citizenship and politics in the new location.

The two communities investigated reflect two groups of minority immigrants in Canada, African Canadians and Latin Americans. The two heritage/museum projects were both in Toronto: the Underground Railroad (UGRR) temporary exhibition held at the Royal Ontario Museum (ROM) in 2002–3, and the Museo de la Solidaridad, a more organic set of exhibitions and activities offered through 2006–7. I undertook interviews with individuals in both organizing groups, and observed and took detailed notes about both exhibitionary media.[1] This chapter links what they were attempting to do through their museum projects to changing ideas about heritage, citizenship, and nation-building in Canada; in other words, how heritage-making through museums becomes a public, communal expression of citizen membership in Canada.

The first case study, the Underground Railroad exhibition at the Royal Ontario Museum, was an exhibit about fugitive slaves who came to Canada from the United States in the mid-nineteenth century. The project was initiated by Canada's National Historic Sites (NHS) as an institutional attempt to bring nontypical users into a mainstream museum space. It was researched, planned, and coproduced with NHS by African Canadians, and successfully attracted both traditional museumgoers (white, educated, middle class) and a range of first-time African Canadians who attended specifically for the show (see Ashley 2011). The second case study is the Museo de la Solidaridad. This is a museum generated from *within* the Chilean community in Toronto (an important difference) to capture and reflect the history, experience, and trauma of Chileans in the context of the struggle for democracy in Latin America. These museum-making activities aimed primarily at newcomer Latin Americans as well as local non-Latino residents. In both cases museum-making by these minority groups appeared to use and rework heritage as a practice of articulating citizenship. The museum sites were used to demand recognition, assert membership, and claim rights in the present and to project a legacy or testimony or colonize the future with their perspectives. But each reflects a different manifestation of this process, one an attempt to present a strategic public face that fits in to the official national heritage of Canada and the other presenting a more multilayered and activist approach that questions or challenges mainstream culture in Canada.

THE UNDERGROUND RAILROAD PROJECT

In the first case study, the committee of African Canadians who developed the Underground Railroad exhibition came from a variety of countries and circumstances. The group represented a complex of identities, allegiances, and power relationships—a range of hyphenated blackness—who expressed their personal sense of heritage in many ways. Several on the exhibit committee, for example, proudly traced their ancestry from fugitive slaves who arrived in Canada in the early 1800s and described a strong sense of legacy as refugees to Canada. Other committee members were recent arrivals from the Caribbean and the United States who described their heritage as Jamaican or American as well as Canadian, and African, and who brought to the table different sets of traditions and sensibilities. For all, a sense of heritage seemed to emerge from complex traditions and narratives of their communities and people, but as well, a shared sense of blackness in relation to the surrounding society in Canada.

The stated intention of this museum-making project was to bring African Canadian heritage on to the public stage in Canada. Despite a long history in Canada, people identified as racially black are subject to subtle and not-so-subtle forms of racism. The committee wanted to dispel myths about their heritage and to assert its legitimacy as part of the national Canadian historical narrative. Their intention was to temper the power of the government institution that sponsored the exhibition by telling their own story. But the positioning of cultural heritage that resulted was highly selective. Committee members had to construct, through heated debate, a public display of collective identity, a unified public face, and this process involved both suppression and overemphasis of certain ideas. The constructedness of history became apparent as they tried to transform their sense of lived heritage into a formal public account of history. They chose to focus on positive black agency, and avoid stories that victimized, but in the process the questions of slavery in Canada and ongoing racism in Canadian society were downplayed. The exhibition employed a range of visual and aural cues to conjure a heartwarming story of survival by a refugee slave woman and the positive aspects of life in Canada. And in the end, the group chose a positive framing—a mainstream public face—a performance that simplified, and mythologized, rather than dwelling on difficult reality (Gable 1996). Audiences received this positive perspective with mixed feelings depending on their motives and backgrounds (Ashley 2011). Some white audience members expressed pride in Canada as a heroic nation, while others took the other extreme and criticized the "whitewash" of the positive story. Most black respondents specifically applauded the upbeat, celebratory tone.

SOLIDARIDAD MUSEUM

The Solidaridad museum took a different tack. It was developed by a group originally from Chile. Most Chileans in Toronto are those who fled their homeland in the wake of the Pinochet military coup in 1973 and took shelter in Canada. These Chileans who arrived as refugees brought their political convictions and social activism, and with it a strong sense of community because of their ideological leftness. Transnational practices have continued to be strong here (back and forth flows of ideas, money, visits) perhaps because of the wealth and intellectual status of these immigrants. Those I interviewed expressed a sense of heritage in terms of the roots or culture, that was passed down to them—the language, attitudes, values, stories, memories, and arts. Ancestors or bloodline figured prominently. Most seemed quite willing to divorce the idea of heritage from any notion of a land base, perhaps an effect of being uprooted. One respondent, interestingly, differentiated between heritage as "matrimony" and heritage as "patrimony." Matrimony for him was a "kith and kin" sense that is part of personal heritage, or the idea of home not necessarily in the sense of a place, but more like "in the bosom of my mother." On the other hand, this respondent defined "patrimony" as a sense of material heritage linked to fatherland—a history, land, wealth, and what the respondent called "the right to control" linking this heritage to formal institutions and power.

The idea of the Solidaridad museum was partially to serve as a community focal point, but also as a political center for Latin Americans in Toronto. In the words of the museum director, here they wanted to "appropriate the museum form to give power to the Latin American community and to validate it through museum-style authority." Solidarity is the name of the museum because that is its intention: to maintain and perpetuate political solidarity with Chileans and other Canadians and to create a legacy to pass on to future generations. Heritage in this case is viewed as having a particular political use of trying to maintain activism. They said they wanted to create a forum, a "contact zone," returning to the past using different forms of art and storytelling, and importantly, hoping to encourage new, multiple, and divergent perspectives about "heritage." For example, they used quilt making to tell political stories, where teens, participating in the traditional craft of quilt making, learned important testimonies from the past, but also, the quilts *they* made became part of an exhibition about the past and future political activism in Canada. The group also felt that museum programs could not only build solidarities among Latin Americans but could also contribute to and build Canadian activism and political participation (or as one said, "to keep the political fighting spirit alive in Canada"). But as well, the museum maintained continual links with cultural groups in Chile and some connection to other transnational activists, a concerted desire to maintain a political and cultural diasporic connection. Audience members participated with varied expectations and motivations, especially because of the activity orientation of the exhibition space. Consequently, participants seemed to derive social, cultural, and/or educational value from their experiences. Those who were most active blended their roles as producers and consumers of heritage, acting out qualities of belonging and membership through their participation.

HERITAGE AND CITIZENSHIP AS PROCESSES OF "MAKING"

While both cases presented here are about museum- and heritage-making among immigrant groups, there are similarities and differences in their approach and attitudes. Both projects have at their core a history of trauma and flight. Both have integrated refugee narratives and subjectivities into their ideas of heritage. Thus in both cases, respondents had moved beyond heritage as a place-based identifier and were seeking other means of signifying the past. Both cases are single-voice museums that might be considered isolating, in terms of participating in the broader public sphere (Brown 1993). In both cases, their exhibitions focused on storytelling, a portable medium that can hold and transfer a sense of heritage more suitably than place or even "things"—there were no collections and few objects here. They voiced a sense of heritage that focused on the immaterial, that incorporated personal stories, songs, and "ways of doing things," rather than thingness or materiality. But in both cases, *creating* concrete manifestations of heritage that embodied their ideas or values became important to the group or community as a strategic act—an exhibit, a museum—solid things as legacy to future generations.

Both groups shared a concern that they were constituted and marginalized by race by other Canadians. The terms African Canadian and Latin American are generalizations that signal racial difference. In each case, these people are not part of homogenous groups but do tend to be constituted this way by government and by other Canadians. The Canadian government imposed blackness on the participants in the UGRR exhibit process by assuming they were dealing with a unitary racial community, and expecting committee members to speak for blacks as a group, even though they came from different parts the world. The Chileans found themselves constituted as Latin American especially within the funding policies of the Department of Canadian Heritage. This "othering" process of identification has been acknowledged by writers in different countries (Piper 1998; Mahtani 2002; Veronis 2007), and in Canada it is sometimes linked to the effects of the national multiculturalism policy, which brackets people into nameable groups then trivializes them as bearers of certain simplistic cultural rites like food and dress (Henry 2002).

But it is in the differences between these two groups that I see possibilities for connecting their activities to new citizenship processes that are not just about status and formal procedures like voting. Formally inscribed ideas of what constitutes citizenship are very often linked in nation-states to particular fixed representations of heritage. Isin and Wood (1999) instead describe a layered conception of citizenship as an active and ongoing process and relationships by which individuals and groups struggle for *rights* rather than a set of formal procedures. I found that both kinds of citizenship were reflected in the heritage-making displayed by my case studies: (1) heritage as a status indicator of nation-state citizenship, and (2), heritage invoked as a part of minority struggles for recognition *in* and active contribution *to* the shaping of Canada.

The Underground Railroad case study hinged on the first: this group wanted to show themselves as a sanctioned part of existing narratives of Canadian-ness, and they "culturalized" any problem areas with a celebratory focus on stories consigned to the distant past. Solidaridad, in contrast, articulated the desire to build political solidarity among different players, and further, to use heritage and creative arts as a process for political action within their new country, Canada. Putnam's distinction between *bonding* and *bridging* social capital is relevant in these different practices of citizenship: bonding interactions are "inward looking and tend to reinforce exclusive identities and homogeneous groups," whereas bridging interactions are "outward looking and encompass people across diverse social cleavages" (Putnam 2000, 22). The committee that produced the black history exhibit actively silenced dissention in their attempt to seek status within the existing social imaginary by reinforcing a superficial positive identity. Solidaridad might be seen instead as a site for heritage practices that could be considered bridging, that draw in different members of Canadian society (other Latins, Anglos, Chileans), seek out new ways to make claims, but more importantly facilitate struggles for dissent and political expression of citizenship. Solidaridad is also an excellent example of a minority group of people making the museum a dialogic "contact zone," in James Clifford's use of the word (1997), as opposed to the African Canadian's reliance on a static transmission of ideas about heritage and citizenship. Thus the two cases reflect divergent approaches to citizenship within these museum-building projects: "mainstreaming" a public face in one case, and asserting power or rights in the other.

But despite these differences in the political nature of the projects, I cannot discount the fact that for the producers of both cases, these committee members I interviewed, there was a strong sense of personal engagement with heritage, and with citizenship. And those people who were committed and engaged emotionally with these museum-building projects demonstrated a very strong sense of heritage and citizenship. They developed wider social networks and communities of practice, more fully participated in the political decision making for "their" communities, and experienced deeper forms of belonging and nuanced senses of heritage than peripheral players and audiences. Thus I would suggest that the very action of "making things public" within these projects enabled, for those who were actively engaged, richer levels of social and cultural capital within their marginalized community and in the broader society. It was not just the representational end product—the museum or exhibition—that was significant for the practice of citizenship in these cases, but the actual process of *creating* these heritage projects. So while I have concluded that while the public face of their museum projects, the actual exhibits that audiences see, expresses two different ways of defining group heritage and expressing group citizenship, on a personal level, *new* imaginings and engagements with heritage and new dynamics of citizenship resulted in the personal lives of those with hands-on involvement in museum-making.

My examples represent the complexity of museum-making, where on one side the objective was to heritage and citizenship as part of and in relation to existing imaginaries of Canada. On the other side, it was more of an assertive process where engagement and creative behavior resisted old imaginaries and proposed new relationships. But I found that was not the only result. Museum-making processes exemplified here can also be seen as useful parts of a cultural tool kit when it comes to expressing and debating identity and membership in a community. What was important was not necessarily the end result—that exhibit or that program, which, by their nature as communication media tend to be fixed in what they can present or perhaps only engage individuals at a single point in time. In fact those fixed end results can sometimes have detrimental or unintended effects. But processes seem key here, the idea of "making" rather than "representation" as the positive knowledge-building and citizen-building connections that museum spaces and practices can offer.

ACKNOWLEDGMENT

Funding for this research was provided through doctoral and postdoctoral fellowships from the Social Sciences and Humanities Research Council of Canada.

NOTES

1. Semistructured interviews were conducted with several individuals involved with production of the exhibits at each site, including planning team members and each project manager (five with the ROM project in 2005 and three with Solidaridad in 2007). The exhibitionary media were observed, described, and analyzed using visual semiotics in 2005 and 2007, respectively. All interviews were conducted in confidentiality, and the names of the interviewees are withheld by mutual agreement.

WORKS CITED

Allen, Garth, and Caroline Anson. 2005. *The Role of the Museum in Creating Multi-Cultural Identities: Lessons from Canada.* Lewiston, NY: Edwin Mellen Press.

Anderson, Benedict. 1983. *Imagined Communities: Reflection on the Origin and Spread of Nationalism.* London: Verso.

Ashley, Susan. 2005. "State Authority and the Public Sphere: Ideas on the Changing Role of Museums as a Canadian Social Institution." *Museum and Society* 3 (1): 5–17.

———. 2011. "Negotiating Narratives of Canada: Circuit of Communication Analysis of the *Next Stop Freedom* Exhibition." *Journal of Canadian Studies / Revue d'études Canadiennes* 45 (2): 182–204.

Ashworth, G. J. 2008. Heritage: Definitions, Delusions, and Dissonances. Keynote Address, Heritage 2008: World Heritage and Sustainable Development Conference, Greenlines Institute, Portugal.

Ashworth, G. J., B. J. Graham, and J. E. Tunbridge. 2007. *Pluralising Pasts: Heritage, Identity, and Place in Multicultural Societies.* London: Pluto Press.

Bennett, Tony. 1995. *The Birth of the Museum: History, Theory, Politics.* London: Routledge.

———. 2006. "Exhibition, Difference, and the Logic of Culture." In *Museum Frictions: Public Cultures/Global Transformations*, edited by I. Karp and C. Kratz, 46–69. Durham, NC: Duke University Press.

Boast, Robin. 2011. "Neocolonial Collaboration: Museum as Contact Zone Revisited." *Museum Anthropology* 34 (1): 56–70.

Bourdieu, Pierre. 1984. *Distinction: A Social Critique of the Judgement of Taste.* Cambridge, MA: Harvard University Press.

Brown, Claudine. 1993. "Community Focused Museums: Reflecting the Reality of a Plurality." *Bulletin of Centre for Museum Studies* 1 (2). www.si.edu/cms/bull/oct93/brown.htm.

Clifford, James. 1997. "Museums as Contact Zones." In *Routes: Travel and Translation in the Late Twentieth Century*, 186–219. Harvard, MA: Harvard University Press.

Duncan, Carol. 1995. "The Art Museum as Ritual." *Art Bulletin* 77: 10–13.

Gable, Eric. 1996. "Maintaining Boundaries, or 'Mainstreaming' Black History in a White Museum." In *Theorizing Museums*, edited by Sharon Macdonald and Gordon Fyfe, 177–201. Oxford: Blackwell.

Gordon-Walker, Caitlin. 2013. "The Process of Chopsuey: Rethinking Multi-cultural Nationalism at the Royal Alberta Museum." In *Diverse Spaces: Identity, Heritage, and Community in Canadian Public Culture*, edited by Susan L. T. Ashley, 16–38. Newcastle-upon-Tyne: Cambridge Scholars Publishing.

Hall, Stuart. 2000. "Whose Heritage? Un-settling 'The Heritage.'" *Third Text* 49: 1–12.

Henry, Frances. 2002. "Canada's Contribution to the 'Management' of Ethno-Cultural Diversity." *Canadian Journal of Communication* 27: 231–42.

Hooper-Greenhill, Eilean. 1992. *Museums and the Shaping of Knowledge.* London: Routledge.

Innis, Harold. 1951. *The Bias of Communication.* Toronto: University of Toronto Press.

Isin, Egin, and Patricia Wood. 1999. *Citizenship and Identity.* London: Sage Publications.

Macdonald, Sharon. 2003. "Museums, National, Postnational, and Transcultural Identities." *Museum and Society* 1 (1): 1–16.

Mahtani, Minelle. 2002. "Interrogating the Hyphen-Nation: Canadian Multi-cultural Policy and 'Mixed Race' Identities." *Social Identities* 8 (1): 67–90.

Message, Kylie. 2009. "New Directions for Civil Renewal in Britain: Social Capital and Culture for All?" *International Journal of Cultural Studies* 12 (3): 257–78.

Peach, Ricardo. 2005. "Trading in Cultural Difference: Diversity and self rep-resentation at the Liverpool Regional Museum, 2000–2003." *Open Museum Journal* 7: 1–26.

Piper, Adrian. 1998. "Passing for White, Passing for Black." In *Talking Visions: Multicultural Feminism in a Transnational Age*, edited by E. Shohat, 75–112. Cambridge, MA: MIT Press.

Putnam, Robert. 2000. *Bowling Alone: The Collapse and Revival of American Community*. New York: Simon and Schuster.

Sandell, Richard 2007. *Museums, Prejudice and the Reframing of Difference*. London: Routledge.

Smith, Laurajane. 2006. *The Uses of Heritage*. London: Routledge.

Smith, Malinda S. 2014. "Commissioning 'Founding Races' and Settler Colonial Narratives." *Canadian Ethnic Studies* 46 (2): 141–49.

Taylor, Charles. 2002. "Modern Social Imaginaries." *Public Culture* 14 (1): 91–124.

Thompson, J. P. 1995. *The Media and Modernity: A Social Theory of the Media*. Stanford, CA: Stanford University Press.

Veronis, Luisa. 2007. "Strategic Spatial Essentialism: Latin Americans' Real and Imagined Geographies of Belonging in Toronto." *Social and Cultural Geography* 8 (3): 455–73.

CONTRIBUTORS

SUSAN L. T. ASHLEY is Senior Lecturer in Cultural Management at Northumbria University. She is a cultural studies scholar interested in the "democratization" of culture and heritage institutions, especially in relation to access and expression by minority groups. Her research on heritage and its relation to subjectivity, representation, and citizenship has been published in books by Routledge and Ashgate, and in peer-reviewed journals such as *Organization, International Journal of Cultural Policy, Museum and Society,* and *International Journal of Heritage Studies.* She edited the volume *Diverse Spaces: Identity, Heritage, and Community,* published in 2013. Dr. Ashley holds a PhD in Communication and Culture from York University, Toronto. She also has twenty years of consultancy and government work coordinating projects for culture and heritage sites across Canada.

TERRI SUSAN FINE is Professor of Political Science at the University of Central Florida, where she also serves as Associate Director and Senior Fellow at the Lou Frey Institute of Politics and Government and as Content Specialist for the Florida Joint Center for Citizenship. Her research has been supported by major grants from the Pew Charitable Trusts, the US Elections Assistance Commission, the US Department of Education, the Florida Department of Education, and Brandeis University Center for the Study of Gender and Judaism. She has published more than thirty articles in refereed journals and edited volumes including *Presidential Studies Quarterly, Polity, Women and Politics, State and Local Government Review,* and the *e-Journal of Public Affairs.*

NORA HUI-JUNG KIM is Associate Professor of Sociology at University of Mary Washington, Fredericksburg, Virginia. Her research interests include international immigration, multiculturalism, race and ethnicity, nationalism, citizenship, and East Asia. She has published in the *International Migration Review, Nations and Nationalism,* and *Citizenship Studies.*

WILL KYMLICKA is the Canada Research Chair in Political Philosophy in the Philosophy Department at Queen's University in Kingston, Canada, where he has taught since 1998. His research interests focus on issues of democracy and diversity, and in particular on models of citizenship and social justice within multicultural societies. He has published eight books and over two hundred articles that have been translated into thirty-two languages.

JOHN O'KEEFE is Assistant Professor of History at Ohio University–Chillicothe, and received his PhD from George Washington University. His current manuscript, titled "Strangers to the Privileges of Citizens: Migrant Influence, Naturalization, and the Growth of National Power over Foreign Migrants in the Early American Republic," examines the role of foreign migrants in the development of citizenship rights during the period after US independence.

ROGERS M. SMITH is the Christopher H. Browne Distinguished Professor of Political Science and Associate Dean for Social Sciences at the University of Pennsylvania, where he also chairs the executive committee of the Penn Program on Democracy, Citizenship, and Constitutionalism. He was elected to the American Academy of Arts and Sciences in 2004 and the American Academy of Political and Social Science in 2011. His research centers on constitutional law, American political thought, and modern legal and political theory, with special interests in questions of citizenship, race, ethnicity, and gender.

KERRY WYNN is Associate Professor of History at Washburn University. Her publications include a related article, "'Miss Indian Territory' and 'Mr. Oklahoma Territory': Marriage, Settlement, and Citizenship in the Cherokee Nation and the United States," in *Moving Subjects: Gender, Mobility, and Intimacy in an Age of Empire,* edited by Tony Ballantyne and Antoinette Burton.

INDEX

www.ingramcontent.com/pod-product-compliance
Lightning Source LLC
Chambersburg PA
CBHW052007270326
41929CB00015B/2826